Merry Christmas, Dad!

♡Hana

TIBET'S HISTORICAL AND CULTURAL LANDSCAPE

Edited by *Wangchen Gelek* and *Chen Qingying*

 FOREIGN LANGUAGES PRESS

First Edition 2006

Translated by Chen Guansheng Li Peizhu

Home Page:
   http://www.flp.com.cn
E-mail Addresses:
   info@flp.com.cn
   sales@flp.com.cn

ISBN 7-119-04203-3

Foreign Languages Press, Beijing, 2006

Published by Foreign Languages Press

24 Baiwanzhuang Road, Beijing 100037, China

Distributed by China International Book Trading Corporation

35 Chegongzhuang Xilu, Beijing 100044, China

P.O. Box 399, Beijing, China

Printed in the People's Republic of China

CONTENTS

Preface

In western China, there is a vast expanse of land. Beautiful and mysterious, it is rich in a variety of natural resources. Here, there are uninterrupted lofty mountain ranges, large rivers, vast areas of grassland, country roads lined with sutra flags, magnificent temples and monasteries, as well as the industrious and brave Tibetan people, who have lived here since ancient times. This is China's Tibetan-inhabited area, the third pole of the planet, with an average altitude of 4,000 meters above sea level. Its full name is the Tibet Autonomous Region, a provincial-level ethnic autonomous region of the People's Republic of China. It occupies the greater part of the Qinghai-Tibet Plateau. Tibet has an area of 1.2 million square kilometers. According to statistics from 1993, the population of the whole region is 2.2888 million. More than 95% of the population are Tibetan, the rest being from the Han, Hui, Monpa, Lhopa, Naxi and Nu peoples. The Tibetan people have lived here generation after generation, created their unique and rich culture through their wisdom and labor, and have made their own brilliant history.

Through their own civilization, the Tibetan people have enriched and developed Chinese civilization. During more than a thousand years of historical development, Tibetan culture has undergone extensive interchanging with that of the Han people and other ethnic groups in China. Tibetans absorbed the fine traditions of other ethnic groups and created a unique culture of their own on the basis of Tibet's natural geographical conditions and sociocultural characteristics. The culture they created became a shining pearl of China's cultural treasure-house. In addition, it greatly influenced other ethnic minorities, such as the Mongols and the Naxi people. Tibetan culture is an important component of overall Chinese culture. The development of Tibetan history and culture fully demonstrates that China's history and culture were created jointly by all of China's ethnic groups.

Since China's policy of reform and opening-up began in the 1980s, the "land of snow" that is Tibet has opened its door to outsiders. Millions of tourists from China and abroad have been to Tibet.

This booklet aims to meet the needs of those who want a publication that combines tourist information and Tibetan history, so that they can understand more deeply and correctly the historical connotations of cultural relics in Tibet. On the basis of a general introduction to Tibetan history in stages, the booklet discusses the cultural relics of each specific stage to help readers gain a more subtle understanding of Tibetan history and culture.

Chapter 1

Inhabitants of the Qinghai-Tibet Plateau in Ancient Times

Prehistoric Tibet and Its Cultural Relics

Tibetan legends and ancient books trace the Tibetan people's ancestors to the ancient inhabitants of the Qinghai-Tibet Plateau. According to the literature of the ancient Tibetan Bön religion, Sipa Sangpo Bontri, the forefather of human beings, was born from a shiny egg and a black egg, which were made up of the five primordial elements (metal, wood, water, fire and

An old legend: the story of the monkey and ogress.

earth). Sipa Sangpo Bontri's descendents were deities of the heavenly realm and earthly realm. They gradually increased in number and became human beings. Another tradition has it that the Tibetan people were the product of the union between a monkey and an ogress and that the ancestors of Tibetans lived on the banks of the Yarlung Zangbo (Brahmaputra River) near Tsethang. This legend might be a product of ancient people's dim memories of their ancestors living in forests.

Ancient Tibetan books say Tibet was controlled by 10 kinds of non-human beings before humans appeared there. At that time, Tibet was called "Bod-kham." The Tibetans have called themselves "Bod-pa" throughout history. This is an example of a place-name changing into the name of an ethnic group. Archaeological findings of recent years, folk legends and myths, and an analysis of the natural environment of the Qinghai-Tibet Plateau suggest that the plateau's ancient people were first active on the forest-covered

land along the middle and lower reaches of the Yarlung Zangbo River. The use of fire later strengthened man's ability to resist wild beasts and led to a greater variety of food. People gradually scattered along the river valleys. They settled along the Yarlung Zangbo, Lhasa, Nyang Chu, Nyang and Yarlung rivers and developed early agriculture and livestock breeding there. The agricultural tribes and nomadic tribes united under the Tubo kingdom and gradually formed the Tibetan ethnic group.

Scenery along the middle and lower reaches of the Yarlung Zangbo River.

Cutting implements from the mid-Paleolithic period.

The Tibetan ethnic group took shape in the same way as ethnic groups elsewhere in the world. In ancient times, the inhabitants of Tibet were grouped into different clans according to blood relationships. Consanguineous clans constituted consanguineous tribes. After a very long period of time, the matrilineal clan society evolved into a patrilineal clan society. According to ancient Tibetan documents, the forefathers of the Tibetan people were divided into four main lineages – Se, Mu, Tong, and Dong. From these four, six minor lineages evolved – Dra, Gru, Dong, Ga, We, and Da. Each lineage has more than 10 subbranches. In Tibetan, the family name is called *rupa*, which literally means "bone" or "of the bone." This shows that family names are closely related to kinship.

As production developed, the population increased and ancient clans migrated, a tribe might be divided into several tribes, or several tribes might merge into one due to intermarriage, the forming of alliances, war or conquest among the tribes. Several tribes might form a league for mutual defense in order to survive the tribal wars over water resources, pasture land, fields, and vassals. Poor and rich appeared. Different social strata also came into being. The chieftains of some tribes became the tribe's aristocracy, and their wealth and power could be passed on to their descendants. Thus, a distinction was made between sovereigns and subjects and between the nobility and the common people. Prisoners of war were treated as slaves, and defeated clans or tribes became dependencies that had to pay tribute or taxes to the victors. Tribal leagues were always breaking up and realigning. Some leagues declined and new leagues arose.

Up to the sixth century AD, there were dozens of tribal leagues on the Tibetan plateau. There were said to have been 40 leagues at first and these then merged into 12 leagues. Of these, there are detailed historical records on only the Pugyal tribe. According to one ancient legend, the first leader of the Pugyal tribe was Nyatri Tsenpo, a youth who descended from the sky to the mortal world at Mount Yarlha Shampo. The herdsmen there made him the tribal chieftain. The youth was ceremoniously given the name Nyatri Tsenpo, "the chieftain seated on a neck throne," because he was brought down the mountain seated on a herdsman's shoulders. Ancient Bön records say that Nyatri Tsenpo was a tribal chieftain after he came to Qonggyai from Bomê, and he was called Pugyal.

According to a Tibetan legend, Yumbulagang was built specially for Nyatri tsenpo as a royal palace. Six generations after Nyatri tsenpo, there was a king named Drigum Tsenpo. He was murdered by Lo-ngam

The Yarlung Valley.

Tazi, one of his subjects. After using deception to murder Drigum tsenpo, the assassin drove the two princes into exile to the Kongpo and Bomê regions, and made himself the tribal chief. Later, Chatri, the second son of Drigum tsenpo, recruited some troops and staged a comeback. After defeating Lo-ngam, he recaptured the throne and held a grand funeral for his father, erecting a mausoleum in the late king's memory. He changed his name to Pude Gungyal and built Chingwa Taktse Castle in Qonggyai.

During the time of Pude Gungyal, people already knew how to produce charcoal, to smelt copper, iron, silver and other kinds of metal, to irrigate farmland and make plows. The emergence of iron farm tools and the use of animal power greatly increased agricultural production, so the population grew and the tribe flourished.

The development of tribal leagues strengthened the power of the *tsenpo* (king). For instance, Nyatri tsenpo had several assistants, who were all tribal chieftains on his mother's side. The distinctive characteristics of the tribal leagues were thus demonstrated. The leaders of all other tribes had to pledge loyalty to the *tsenpo*. Their position, territory, and subjects were considered to be gifts from the *tsenpo*. If they were disloyal, the *tsenpo* could deprive them of their fief and subjects.

By the time of Takbu Nyesik, the 29th generation of *tsenpo*, the Yarlung Pugyal tribe had fundamentally unified the southern bank of the Yarlung Zangbo River and was trying to expand its power to the northern bank. An authentic account of the annexation as recorded in ancient Tibetan manuscripts was found in the Dunhuang caves. In about the sixth century AD, there were two local regimes in the Lhasa valley. One was in Drigung and its chief was called Takgyawo. The other was in Phanpo to the north of Lhasa and its chief was Tripansong. Takbu Nyesik of the Pugyal tribe secretly supported Tripansong in his annexation of Takgyawo's tribe. Later, Takbu Nyesik made use of conflicts between

Tripansong on the one hand and the Shan and Wei family, two slave-owning aristocrats from the Tripansong tribe, on the other, to plot the annexation of the Tripansong tribe. At that time, the Nyang, Tsepangsa, Wei and Lun families formed an alliance. These four clans and Takbu Nyesik pledged alliance to one another. When they were about to set off on a military expedition, Takbu Nyesik died of an illness. His son, Namri Lontsen, continued the expedition after ascending the throne. Namri Lontsen had the Nyang and Lun clans act as military spies and the Wei and Tsepangsa clans act as guides. He himself led an army of 10,000 soldiers to conquer the Tripansong tribe. After annexing Tripansong, Namri Lontsen gave 1,500 slaves to each of the Nyang, Wei and Lun clans, while giving 300 slaves to the Tsepangsa clan.

Having conquered the Lhasa area, Namri Lontsen captured Shigatse (Xigazê) in the Tsang region, killed the local chief, seized the land there and the valuables of 20,000 households and took control of the Shigatse area. By that time, the Pugyal tribe had unified the middle and lower reaches of the Yarlung Zangbo River – that is, the main agricultural area of Tibet.

Tibet's prehistoric period covers the time when human beings began to develop a civilization on the Tibet Plateau before the establishment of the Tubo Dynasty. The plateau's inhabitants created a brilliant ancient civilization and left behind a precious cultural heritage. The cultural landscape of this period includes several remains of the ancient Tibetans, such as the Karub cultural site in Qamdo County, the Qoigong site in Lhasa, and the Yumbulagang palace built in the Yarlung valley by Nyatri tsenpo, the first tsenpo or king of the Pugyal tribe. There are also many ancient stone implements and rock paintings created by the highland area's inhabitants. Most of these ancient cultural relics have been excavated since the 1970s.

Karub Archaeological Site (Karub village in Qamdo County)

The Karub site was discovered in the village of Karub in Tibet's Qamdo County, hence the name. It dates back 4,000 years to Neolithic times and covers an area of 10,000 square meters.

An initial excavation uncovered a variety of ancient artifacts at the archaeological site, including 31 house foundations and a storage pit. There are two kinds of houses – those made of grass and earth and those with stone walls. The stone-walled houses had two stories and were partially underground, with a stove or fireplace inside. Altogether, 7,968 chipped stone tools, tiny blade tools and polished stone tools were found, including spades, axes, hoes, plows, and tools for cutting, scraping or chopping. More than 400 bone implements were unearthed, including awls and needles,

Painted twin-bodied pottery bottles unearthed from the Karub archaeological site in Qamdo.

as were more than 20,000 pieces of pottery jars, bowls, and painted pots in four colors – red, yellow, gray and black. Bones from about a dozen different kinds of animals – such as pigs, antelopes and roe deer – were excavated at the Karub site, as well as a large quantity of ash from millet and other grains. The Karub archaeological site provides evidence that the primitive aborigines were gradually abandoning their nomadic lifestyle to settle down and that their productive activities were expanding from hunting and foraging to farming and animal husbandry. Archaeologists believe that the Karub site was a primitive village that lasted for at least a thousand years, that the Karub culture was basically at the same level as the Majiayao and Banshan cultures and the Machang culture of the Yellow River valley, and that there were great similarities between these cultures.

The precious remains of the Karub culture vividly demonstrate the lives of ancient people on the Qinghai-Tibet Plateau. By that time, people had already given up living in caves as hunter-gatherers and they had begun to build houses and had learned how to make pottery for storing water or cooking. Their productive activities were not limited to fishing and hunting. They grew grain and raised domestic livestock as subsidiary activities. They could make wild hemp into thread with a pottery spinning wheel, and then weave coarse cloth out of the thread. They sewed the cloth into simple clothes. By that time, people already had a nascent aesthetic judgment and they had fashioned bone needles, bone bracelets, stone rings and stone beads for ornaments. They pierced a hole in shells, strung them together with thread, and used these to adorn their bodies. Judging from the foundations of the houses that have been excavated, family units had already emerged, and primitive society had entered its later period.

Qoigong Archaeological Site (Lhasa)

The Qoigong site dates back to the Neolithic age. It is in the northern suburbs of Lhasa, to the west of the renowned Sera Monastery and about 5 kilometers north of central Lhasa. The site is about 150 meters wide from east to west and about 30 meters long from north to south, and it has a total area of about 5,000 square meters. The first excavation of the site took place in 1984. Great discoveries were made also in the second excavation in 1990.

There are two ancient stone-plate tombs and about a dozen ash pits at the site. About 10,000 stone tools have been unearthed. The bone tools that have been unearthed have been made of animal limb bones, finely polished. The tools include needles and awls. Special attention should be paid to a bone needle whose hole is near the point instead of at the other end. It is the first such bone needle to have been unearthed from a prehistoric site in

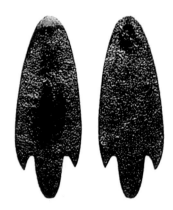

Bronze arrowheads unearthed from the Qoigong archaeological site.

China. It seems to have had a different function than the other needles, and looks like the needle of a modern sewing machine.

Stone shovels and stone querns (hand mills) have been unearthed, which indicates that primitive farming culture already existed in the area around Lhasa some 4,000 years ago.

The unearthed pottery tools show good workmanship. There are numerous shapes: jars with one ear, jars with two ears, and pots with long necks and big bellies. Geometric patterns have been carved on the polished surfaces. All the pottery tools unearthed at Qoigong were handmade. Most of them are gray in color, with others being black, brown or red-brown, and they all have a polished surface. The pottery decorations were carved into the wet clay. There are trellis patterns, triangle patterns, lineal wave patterns, and geometric design, among others. Most of the pottery items are jars, but there are also pots with round bottoms, bowls, *dou* (stemmed bowls), and ewers. The Qoigong site provides evidence that Lhasa was one of the important areas where the ancestors of today's Ti-

Copper mirror with an iron handle, unearthed from the Qoigong archaeological site.

betans lived as early as 4,000 years ago. This is of great significance for the study of the Tibetan people's early history.

Ngunda Archaeological Site (Ngunda village in Qamdo township)

The Ngunda site is one of the important Neolithic sites discovered by Tibetan archaeologists in the past few years. It is near the village of Ngunda by the Ngom Qu river, 4 kilometers from Qamdo township in Qamdo Prefecture. The site is 3,200 meters above sea level, with an area of about 10,000 square meters. An investigation and a partial trial excavation in 1986 resulted in a great amount of relics being unearthed: lumps of burnt earth, large chipped stone tools, microliths (tiny blade tools), polished stone tools, bone tools, broken pieces of pottery, charcoal ash, and so on. Among the relics were 52 large chipped stone tools, seven microliths, 11 polished stone tools, 20 bone tools, and 14 broken pieces of pottery. The large chipped stone tools are all made of sandstone or hornstone and comprise three cores, 25 flakes, 13 chopping tools, four pointed implements, one hammer and six scraping tools. The microliths are all of black flint and comprise one core, three flakes, one scraping tool and two pointed implements. The polished stone tools comprise three stone adzes and nine stone knives. The broken pieces of handmade pottery are of sandstone and are gray or red. The clay of the pottery is porous and the firing method did not use a high enough temperature. The decorative designs on the pottery include incised and embossed decorations. It is estimated that the Ngunda site is from about the same period as the Karub site – that is, between 4,000 and 5,000 years ago.

When the trial excavation at Ngunda took place in 1986, a tomb was discovered. The tomb chamber was built with stone plates, to form a rectangular stone coffin. It was a flexed burial (with the body buried in the fetal position). A human skeleton and a pottery jar with two ears were unearthed. The pottery jar is 14.3 centimeters tall, and the diameter of its mouth is 9.9 centimeters. It is a handmade gray sandstone jar, with a flared mouth, short neck, big belly and flat bottom, with two long ears at the neck. On the jar's belly and ears are leaf-vein designs. Archaeologists believe the stone coffin burial is from a period dating after the Karub culture. A tentative estimate made in 1986 dated the tomb to 3,905 years previously – that is, 1,919 BC. The archaeological culture it represents was first discovered in Tibet and is of very great academic significance.

Tibetan Rock Pictures (at Gyaling in the Nagchu area, Rutog in the Ngari area, Dingri County etc)

Most ancient Tibetan rock pictures are distributed in the highlands of northwestern and northern Tibet at altitudes of more than 4,500 meters along the middle and upper reaches of the Yarlung Zangbo River. Quite a few rock pictures are in areas that are now unpopulated. The rock pictures are widely scattered and differ in date and style, although the styles are broadly similar. The pictures are characteristic of the rock art of northern China and their style is rough, vigorous, simple and strong. At the same time, they have unique distinguishing features of the highland regions.

Tibetan rock pictures were mainly made by chipping and rubbing. They cover a wide range of subjects, including primitive religion, trade, Bön sacrificial rites and symbols of the Bön faith. The Gyaling pictures in northern Tibet, the Rimdong pictures in Rutog and the Chiwup picture site in Ngari are the most representative. Tibetan rock pictures may be divided into three periods: (1) All the rock pictures of the first period depict scenes of herding and hunting of some 4,000 to 5,000 years ago, before the rise of Bön culture. The Gyaling pictures in northern Tibet and those at Monje in Dingri County are representative of this period. Most of the pictures show the herding of sheep and cattle, hunting, and the taming of wild yaks. (2) The rock pictures of the second period are of western Tibet's ancient Shangshung civilization of about 1,000 BC, during the early period of Bön culture. They depict primitive nature worship, genital worship, sorcery, and symbols of the Bön faith. The Chiwup and Rimdong rock pictures are representative of this period. (3) The rock pictures of the third period have a unique style and are from a later period. The pictures' subject matter involves hunting and animals. The animals in these kinds of pictures include oxen, sheep, deer, and dogs. On the animals' bodies, there is always an S shape or a spiral pattern, with distinctive decorative features.

Rock paintings at Sera Monastery.

A rock painting of Tsongkhapa in Drepung Monastery.

Yumbulagang (Nedong County in Shannan Prefecture)

Yumbulagang.

Yumbulagang is about five kilometers southeast of Nedong County, on a hilltop on the eastern bank of the Yarlung River. According to Tibetan legends, it was Tibet's first royal palace and was built in the first century BC for Nyatri tsenpo, the chieftain of the Yarlung tribe. *Yumbu* means "mother and son," while *lagang* means "palace," so Yumbulagang is the "Mother and Son Palace." At the time of Songtsen Gampo, two two-story buildings were built on each side of the original palace building. The ground floors comprised halls for worshiping Buddha and the upper stories halls for worshiping Dharma-raja, the King of the Law (Sakyamuni). Thus, Yumbulagang ceased to be used as a dwelling and became a temple. This tall, dignified building rises erect on the spur of a hill, commanding an impressive view of the entire valley.

Yumbulagang.

The Yumbulagang building complex may be divided into three groups:

(1) The fortress-like building: Tibetan legend says this part of the building is the original one built for Nyatri tsenpo. It is in the center of the eastern section and is 11 meters high, with a length of 4.6 meters from north to south and a width of 3.5 meters from east to west. The lower part is larger than the upper part. From the outside, it looks like a five-story building but it actually has three stories. The ground floor is 1.2 meters high. The middle story has a hall with a small entrance at the top, and the third story used to have a gilded roof made by the fifth Dalai Lama. The building has very thick walls and the interior is small.

(2) The great hall: Tradition has it that Songtsen Gampo made the hall. It had three stories in the past but the number of stories was reduced to two when it was renovated. All the statues in the hall were destroyed during the Cultural Revolution (1966-76). Along the back wall of the hall, there are now several bronze statues, including Maitreya, Manjusri, Tsongkhapa, Tara, and Padmasambhava. On the shelves on the western side are the Buddhist *Kangyur* scriptures. On the eastern side of the room is a mural depicting the earliest events in Tibetan history. Nyatri tsenpo is shown descending from the heavens and settling into an early form of the Yumbulagang. A Buddhist scripture is seen descending from the sky during the time of King Lhatotori Nyantsen and falling onto Yumbulagang's tower. In the back corridor, there is a passageway leading to the fortress-like building.

(3) The monks' dormitory and its adjacent room: The monks' dormitory is south of the great hall. The room is on the upper floor, near the great hall. It used to be the Dalai Lama's bedroom but has been renovated.

The hall has exquisitely carved statues of all the Tubo Dynasty *tsenpos* (kings) and Princess Wencheng and Princess Bhrikuti Devi (also known as Tritsun). Many historic cultural relics and classic writings are also preserved here.

Chapter 2

The Jokhang Temple

The Brilliant Tubo Dynasty and the Introduction of Buddhism

After Namri Lontsen unified the middle and lower reaches of the Yarlung Zangbo River, he set up another ruling center in the Lhasa Valley in addition to Chingwa Taktse, the Pugyal tribe's capital. This was so he could more effectively control the areas he had newly occupied. Tibetan historical documents state that his son Songtsen Gampo was born in Yarlung Tadul in Maizhokunggar and succeeded to the throne at the age of 13. Therefore, Namri Lontsen must have been on the throne for more than a decade after he had subdued all the neighboring small kingdoms. During this time, his main activities obviously were waging war against the remaining forces of resistance and continuing his unification wars against neighboring kingdoms such as the Sumpa and Shangshung. At the same time, he had to harmonize relations between old and new aristocrats to solve the contradictions caused by the uneven distribution of power among them. He also had to strengthen the position of the *tsenpo* and consolidate the new ruling dynasty's power.

As soon as Songtsen Gampo ascended the throne at the age of 13, he took

Songtsen Gampo (in the Potala)

a series of resolute measures to suppress rebellious forces and eliminate opponents. He adopted various policies to consolidate the Tubo regime and played a great role in Tibetan history. He is therefore considered the founder of the Tubo Dynasty.

Songtsen Gampo's achievements may be grouped into three areas: (1) Creation of the Tibetan script and the promulgation of laws.

Some incomplete scripts may have been used before Songtsen Gampo came to power. However, not long after he came to power, he sent his minister Thonmi Sambhota together with a group of young aristocrats to India to study Sanskrit and phonetics. After returning to Tibet, Thonmi Sambhota created an alphabet. Songtsen Gampo widely advocated it and took the lead in using it. The alphabet later became popular among the Tibetan people and is the Tibetan script still in use today. The creation of the Tibetan script promoted the development and diffusion of Tibetan culture.

Songtsen Gampo formulated a series of laws to more effectively administer the whole of Tibet. He appointed high-ranking central government officials. Under the *tsenpo* were four leading ministers: a chief minister (called the Senior Lon), an assistant minister (called the Junior Lon), a grand marshal and a deputy grand marshal. These four ministers helped the *tsenpo* with administration. The Senior Lon was the highest official. He ranked second only to the *tsenpo* and was higher-ranking than all the other officials. It was stipulated that all officials were to be classified into 12 grades and that they should wear badges of different materials to show their different ranks. In descending order of rank, the badges were made of *sese* (precious stones), gold, gilded silver, silver, copper, iron, and so on. People were divided into different social strata. The values attached to the lives of those in different grades were not the same. The figure might vary from 11,000 ounces down to 10 ounces of silver. If someone from a lower class killed someone from a higher class, the murderer would be put to death, as well as having his property confiscated. After the classification of social classes received the protection of the law, the role played by blood relationships inside the clan was weakened, and the king's authority was eventually solidly established.

(2) Establishment of the system of civil and military officials.

Songtsen Gampo divided the middle and lower reaches of the Yarlung Zangbo River into four *ru* or divisions: Wuru (central region, with its seat in modern Lhasa), Yoru (left wing, with its seat in Nedong), Yeru (right wing, with its center in modern Namling) and Rulag (sub-wing, with its seat in what is now Lhazê). A *ru* comprised an upper and a lower sub-*ru*. Each of these two subdivisions was governed by a marshal and a deputy general. Every subdivision had four civil offices and one guard office each in charge of a thousand households. *A Feast for Wise Men* says that each *ru* had a royal guard office in charge of a thousand households and this was directly controlled by the *tsenpo*. The four *ru* thus had a total of 40 offices each in charge of a thousand households. After subduing Shangshung and Sumpa, 10 such offices were set up in Shangshung and 11 in Sumpa. By then, there were 61 such offices in the whole of Tubo. Every one of these offices had its own chief, appointed by the *tsenpo*.

The living quarters of Songtsen Gampo and Princess Wencheng in Pabongka Temple.

Ministers with conspicuous merit might be appointed hereditary chiefs in charge of these offices.

Tubo was divided on the basis of districts instead of clans into the four *ru* and the thousand-household offices. Therefore, the *ru* and thousand-household offices were administrative organs of the dynasty and were not based on tribal blood relationships. Each thousand-household office comprised a number of tribes. Every tribe had its own chieftain, military officer, tax collector and civil official, and they were in charge of managing what the tribe produced, military affairs, taxes and so on. Judging from documents discovered in Dunhuang and the Tibetan-inscribed wooden slips of the Tubo period discovered in Xinjiang, it was common for there to be several surnames in a single tribe. Some tribes even had immigrants from other ethnic groups. This shows that, during the Tubo Dynasty, tribes were also changing into administrative organs.

(3) Continued unification of the Qinghai-Tibet Plateau.

After conquering Shangshung and Sumpa, the newly established Tubo Dynasty continued its northeastward territorial expansion. The north of the Tubo area bordered the Tuyuhun area around Lake Qinghai. The Tuyuhun royal family came from the Xianbei ethnic group of northeastern China, while the subjects under its control in Qinghai were mostly members of the Qiang ethnic group. To open up a passageway to the economically and culturally developed Yellow River valley, Tubo tried hard to annex Tuyuhun. Songtsen Gampo led his troops, together with those of Shangshung, in an attack on Tuyuhun and occupied a large part of its territory. The Tuyuhun rulers asked the Tang Dynasty for help. Mili-

Princess Wencheng (in the Potala)

Tang Dynasty zither-like musical instrument taken to Tibet by Princess Wencheng—36-string *qin*.

tary conflict thus broke out between Tubo and the newly established Tang Dynasty. Songtsen Gampo personally led an army in a siege of Songzhou (now Songpan in Sichuan Province). But victory was proving elusive in the war, so Songtsen Gampo sent envoys to the Tang court with a proposal for a marriage alliance in an attempt to establish friendly relations with the Tang rulers.

As a man of great talent and bold vision, Songtsen Gampo clearly made great contributions to the establishment and unification of Tubo. At the same time, he made great efforts to expand economic and cultural exchanges with neighboring countries. First, he sent his minister Gar Tongtsen as an envoy to Nepal to escort Princess Bhrikuti Devi (Tritsun) to Lhasa. In 640, he again sent Gar Tongtsen to Chang'an (now Xi'an in Shaanxi Province) to propose marriage between Songtsen Gampo and a Tang princess. After great efforts by all concerned, Emperor Taizong promised Princess Wencheng's hand in marriage to the Tubo *tsenpo*. In 641, Princess Wencheng went to Tibet as a bride-to-be, accompanied by Li Daozong, the Prince of Jiangxia. Songtsen Gampo and his followers greeted her at the source of the Yellow River. This shows that he attached great importance to the arrival of Princess Wencheng.

six-string *qin*.

The arrival in Tibet of Princess Bhrikuti Devi and Princess Wencheng increased Tubo's economic and cultural contacts with southern Asia and the central plains. Many productive skills and handicrafts were introduced to Tubo and books on medicine, almanacs and books on arithmetic were brought there, which helped Tubo develop economically and culturally. Both Princess Bhrikuti Devi and Princess Wencheng were Buddhists. Legend has it that Princess Wencheng brought many statues of Buddha and many Buddhist monks to Tibet. The two princesses had the Jokhang Temple and Ramoche Temple built in Lhasa for the images of Buddha they had brought to Tibet. The two temples are among the earliest Buddhist temples built in Tibet. Songtsen Gampo also had the Tritse Marpo palace built on Red Hill (Hong Shan), the site of today's Potala. It shows the architectural artistry of the early Tubo Dynasty. Princess Wencheng, who died in 680, lived in Tubo for nearly 40 years and the events of her life have been widely known in Tibetan-inhabited areas for the past thousand years and more.

Following the marriage of Songtsen Gampo and Princess Wencheng, political relations between the Tubo and Tang dynasties improved greatly. In 645, Tang Emperor Taizong returned to his capital city of Chang'an after a successful campaign against Korea, following which Songtsen Gampo sent his minister Gar Tongtsen to Chang'an to express congratulations and offer a gift of a golden goose seven *chi* ($2^1/_3$ meters) high.

In 648, the Tang emissary Wang Xuance was attacked on his way to Sindhu (in modern-day India) by an armed gang from that region. He and his party withdrew into the Tubo area. At the Tang official's request, Songtsen Gampo promptly dispatched a contingent of troops to rout the marauders. Ten years later, Wang Xuance again went to Sindhu by way of Tubo. The cliff carving *Record of the Great Tang Emissary to Sindhu* is still preserved in Tibet's Gyirong County, serving as a historical witness of the friendly relationship between the Tang and Tubo dynasties at that time.

The Tang Emperor Taizong died in 649. When the new Tang emperor, Gaozong, came to the throne, he conferred on the Tibetan *tsenpo* the office of Imperial Son-in-Law Governor, with the honorific title Prince of the Western Region. Thus honored, Songtsen Gampo wrote to the Tang court pledging his allegiance. To commend the Tibetan *tsenpo*'s loyalty, Emperor Gaozong gave him the new title of Treasured Prince. Gaozong also had a stone statue carved of the Tibetan king and had it put at Emperor Taizong's tomb to show his great esteem for the Tubo *tsenpo*.

Songtsen Gampo died in 650. As his son Gungsong Gungtsen had already died, he was succeeded to the throne by his grandson Mangsong Mangtsen, who was only a child at the time. Therefore, Gar Tongtsen, Songtsen Gampo's trusted minister, acted as regent until the boy came of age. Gar Tongtsen continued Songtsen Gampo's policies, perfected legislation, carried out checks on residents, drew up a criterion for taxation, and pacified the interior of Tubo. He led troops several times to attack Tuyuhun by exploiting internal conflicts there, for which he even risked coming into conflict with the Tang court.

After Gar Tongtsen died in 667, his sons held positions of power in the Tubo Dynasty. To support Tuyuhun, the Tang court sent more than 100,000 troops to escort the king of Tuyuhun back to Qinghai in 670. Gar Trinring mustered 200,000 troops to meet the approaching Tang troops and defeated them at Dafeichuan to the south of Lake Qinghai. The Tang army was routed. The area around Lake Qinghai was then under Tubo's firm control. Tubo began to contend for Longyou and the Hexi Corridor (in today's Gansu Province) and the four garrisons of Anxi (in Xinjiang) in an attempt to control the Silk Road for economic benefit.

In 676, the Tibetan ruler Mangsong Mangtsen died. His son was born shortly after his death. This son, Dusong Mangpoje, was chosen to be the *tsenpo* but Gar Trinring still had power in his hands. Due to the fact that the Gar family was in control for a long time, contradictions developed between the Gar family and other aristocratic families. Furthermore, the continuous growth of the Gar family's military power and the family's unruliness constituted a formidable challenge to the royal house's centralized authority. Therefore, Dusong Mangpoje took drastic measures when he reached maturity. From 695 to 698, he led an expedition to Qinghai, where Trinring had stationed his forces. In 698, Trinring's army was defeated and he committed suicide. Trinring's younger brother, Gar Tsenba, and Tsenba's son Lon Mangpoje surrendered to the Tang court together with their followers.

After Dusong Mangpoje had liquidated Gar Trinring's forces, the Tubo *tsenpo*'s power was strengthened and consolidated. Shortly after, in 704, Dusong Mangpoje led a large army into Yunnan to subdue the Nanzhao kingdom, but he died the following year before the end of the expedition. Tride Tsugtsen, who was only seven years old at the time, succeeded his father to the throne but his grandmother, Trimalo, acted as regent until he became an adult. By the later period of Empress Wu Zetian's reign, the Tang and Tubo dynasties had become weak because of frequent wars and they both hoped to restore peaceful and friendly relations. While Dusong Mangpoje was still alive, Trimalo sent envoys to the Tang court with a proposal for a marriage alliance. After his death, she again sent envoys to seek matrimonial

A fresco of Princess Jincheng in the Potala.

links with the Tang royal house for Tride Tsugtsen. Wu Zetian died in 705 and the Tang Emperor Zhongzong succeeded to the throne. He promised to give the *tsenpo* the hand in marriage of Princess Jincheng, the daughter of Prince Yong, Li Shouli. In 710, Emperor Zhongzong sent his own envoys together with Tubo special envoys to escort Princess Jincheng to Tibet. With his officials, the Tang emperor himself escorted the princess to Shiping County in today's Shaanxi Province and held a farewell party there. At the Tubo envoys' request, the emperor bestowed Jiuqu in the Hexi Corridor on Princess Jincheng. The princess brought with her to Tibet a great many artisans, acrobats, musicians and Buddhist monks. All of this played an important role in the development of the Tubo economy and culture. After Princess Jincheng went to Tibet, both sides maintained peaceful relations for a period of time.

In 731, Tride Tsugtsen and Princess Jincheng sent envoys to request various classic writings and history books such as *The Book of Songs*, *The Book of Rites* and the *Zuo Zhuan* (*Zuo Supplement to the Spring and Autumn Annals*) from the Tang emperor, and Tubo asked for the border to be defined and for trade to be encouraged. Thus, in 733, the Tang and Tubo held a conference in the Chiling mountain range (now the Riyue Shan range in Qinghai Province's Huangyuan County), at which both sides agreed to establish the border along the Chiling range and to open up markets for trade in Gansongling (now Songpan in Sichuan Province) and Chiling. The Tang and Tubo border generals attended the meeting. It was announced to them that, from that day on, the Tang and Tubo dynasties would have good relations and would not harass each other.

War broke out again between the Tang and Tubo dynasties not long afterward because the ruling groups on both sides wanted to expand their power and influence and because the border generals wanted to earn greater merit with their lords. The Tubo Dynasty made an alliance with the Durgyis to the north and united with the Nanzhao kingdom in Yunnan to the southeast. In 751, the Nanzhao king pledged allegiance to the Tubo Dynasty. The Tubo Dynasty thus succeeded in making the Nanzhao kingdom its dependency, and it conferred on the king of Nanzhao, Geluofeng, the royal title of Tsenpo Drong (Tibetan for "the *tsenpo*'s brother"). With the Nanzhao kingdom as its dependency, the Tubo Dynasty became stronger and imposed a direct threat in southwestern China to the Tang Dynasty.

As the war dragged on, some generals became very powerful and rebellious. In 754, the Tubo ruler Tride Tsugtsen was assassinated by two of his ministers, Bal Dongtsap and Langme Zig. The Tubo royal house put down the rebellion a year later, and Trisong Detsen, who was only 13 years old, ascended the throne in 755. It was in this year that the relative military strengths of the Tang and Tubo dynasties changed drastically. In 755, the An Lushan/Shi Siming Rebellion broke out. The Tang Emperor Xuanzong fled from the capital city of Chang'an to Sichuan in utter confusion. The war of rebellion greatly weakened the Tang Dynasty's strength and prestige. This was especially true after the Tang court recalled the garrison troops from the western borders and sent them to fight the rebels. Taking advantage of the Tang Dynasty's unguarded western borders, the Tubo Dynasty launched a large-scale offensive against the Tang. Almost the entire Hexi Corridor and Longyou were thus lost to the Tubo, except for a few places still held by Tang troops. In October 763, some 200,000 Tubo troops broke through the Tang's defensive line and stormed their way into Chang'an. The Tang Emperor Daizong fled to Shanzhou. The Tubo installed Li Chenghong (Princess Jincheng's nephew) as the new Tang emperor. After sacking the city for 15 days, the Tubo troops retreated westward. The Tubo Dynasty expanded greatly its territory after the war led by Trisong Detsen.

Rituals being performed during a Buddhist assembly.

Although there were conflicts and wars between the Tang and Tubo, these did not prevent the Han and Tibetan peoples from having friendly contact and economic and cultural exchanges. Silk, tea and other goods gradually became everyday household goods for the Tibetans, while copious amounts of animal products and medicine flowed into the central plains. Tubo costumes, decorations, craftwork and the sport of polo all had a certain influence on the Tang court.

Buddhism played a very important role in the later period of Tubo history. During Songtsen Gampo's reign, Buddhism began to penetrate Tibet, and serious conflict arose over whether it was advisable to believe in Buddhism. A century later, the Tubo ruler Trisong Detsen came to the throne and wiped out those ministers who were devoted to the Bön religion and strongly opposed to Buddhism. At his invitation, the Indian Buddhist master Shantarakshita (known as Shiwatso in Tibetan) and the great Tantric master Padmasambhava went to Tibet and spread the religion far and wide. Padmasambhava was renowned for his suppression and conversion of malevolent spirits and hostile non-Buddhist forces. He absorbed all the non-Buddhist spirits into esoteric Buddhism and set up a whole set of sacrificial rituals for people to worship them in order to propagate Buddhism more smoothly in Tubo society. The two Indian masters built Samye Monastery between 767 and 779 and this was the first Buddhist monastery in Tibet. Trisong Detsen selected seven intelligent men to be trained by Shantarakshita, and they became the first monks in Tibet. Many other youths from aristocratic families were encouraged to become monks, and this laid a solid foundation for the spread of Buddhism. From then on, Buddhism developed rapidly in Tubo. Trisong Detsen and his successors Muni Tsenpo and Tride Songtsen spared no effort in their patronage of Buddhism. All of the Buddhist monasteries and monks enjoyed the patronage of the royal house and were supported with the taxes paid by the general public. The monasteries and monks spontaneously came under the control of the royal house.

After Tride Songtsen's son Tritsug Detsen (also known as Ralpachen) ascended the throne in 815, he took the policy of patronizing Buddhism further by building temples, increasing the number of monks, and translating Buddhist scriptures on a large scale. To encourage people to become monks, Ralpachen decreed that every seven households would have to provide for the needs of one monk and that, if anybody committed any offence against Buddhists, the *tsenpo* would severely punish the culprit. However, this state of affairs did not last for long. The *tsenpo*'s devotion to Buddhism increased the contradictions between the monks and lay people and between different political cliques. Ralpachen was eventually murdered by two of his ministers who were bitterly opposed to the Buddhist religion. His brother Lang Darma was put on the throne by ministers opposed to Buddhism and so Lang Darma followed their advice.

In 843, Lang Darma ordered the closure of all Buddhist temples and monasteries in Tubo, compelled all monks to leave their religious orders, and burned Buddhist scriptures. He destroyed and buried Buddhist images. He even ordered the monks to become hunters and butchers. Lang Darma's powerful persecution only met fierce resistance by the monks. Finally, in 846, Lang Darma was assassinated by Lhalung Palgye Dorje, a monk set on revenge.

After Lang Darma died, the nobles soon split into two groups, each backing one of the king's two sons Yumtan and Osung in the contest for the throne. At the same time, the Tubo generals in the outlying regions were also locked in armed strife against each other. This led to the destruction of the forces of social production and sharpened social contradictions. A large-scale rebellion of slaves broke out in Tubo. The rebellion did not have a unified leadership but covered a large area. Shortly after the rebellion, the rebels declared that they would kill all officials of the Tibetan king. The slave uprising made the Tubo Dynasty collapse completely.

The Tubo Dynasty was the first unified Tibetan regime. It had a complete system for political, economic, and cultural administration. It unified various independent tribes on the Tibet Plateau and had contacts with all the neighboring countries and ethnic groups. This period may be regarded as the first time when Tibet really flourished. During the Tubo Dynasty, the Tibetan script was created and this is still in use today; laws and regulations with strong local characteristics were promulgated; and Buddhism was introduced into Tibet. Therefore, the culture of this period had prominent Tibetan characteristics. Major landmarks from this time include well-known monasteries and temples such as Samye Monastery, Jokhang Temple, Ramoche Temple and Trandruk Temple, as well as murals, grottoes, cliff paintings, and the Tang-Tubo alliance tablet, which reflects the close ties of the two sides. The Ti-

betan documents and murals discovered at Dunhuang, although this was not an area under Tubo jurisdiction, are representative of Tibetan culture in the Tubo period and so are of special significance.

Jokhang Temple (Lhasa)

The Jokhang Temple is in the center of the old city of Lhasa and is now a key cultural site under state protection. It is considered the most sacred temple in Tibet. It is more than 1,300 years old, construction having begun in 647 after Songtsen Gampo married his

The Jokhang Temple.

Nepalese wife Bhrikuti Devi (Tritsun) and his Han Chinese wife Wencheng. Legend has it that, before the temple was built, Princess Wencheng perceived the form of a female demon in Tibet's landscape and, to subdue the demon, formed the idea of building temples on the most prominent parts of the demon's body. The Jokhang was built on the site of a lake that a sacred goat had previously filled with earth. The queen thought this site was the demon's heart. The temple was originally called Trulnang Tsuklakhang. Later, the Jowo Sakyamuni statue that Wencheng took to Tibet was moved to this temple by Princess Jincheng. The temple was then given its present name of Jokhang, meaning the "Shrine of the Jowo." According to Tibetan sources, the Jokhang Temple took 12 months to build but it was not then a large-scale

The Jokhang Temple's Jowo Sakyamuni statue, which Princess Wencheng took to Tibet.

The Jokhang Temple.

Religious decorations on the Jokhang Temple.

The Jokhang Temple entrance.

Jokhang Temple eaves.

temple. It had eight halls during the Tang period. Extension projects carried out during the Yuan, Ming and Qing dynasties expanded it to its present size, with a total area of about 25,000 square meters. The Jokhang was considerably enlarged and embellished during the reign of the fifth Dalai Lama in particular. The Kashag (the Tibetan local government) had its offices in the Jokhang, beginning in the reign of the seventh Dalai Lama.

The Jokhang Temple is a combination of Han and Tibetan architectural skill. For instance, the roof beams and the system of brackets inserted between the tops of the main hall's columns and crossbeams are in a Han style, while the eaves and the tops of the pillars are decorated in a typical Tibetan style with bright colors and sharp contrasts. There are many precious cultural relics in the Jokhang, such as the Jowo Sakyamuni statue, embroidered images of Buddha dating from the Tang Dynasty, huge silver lamps from the Yuan Dynasty, a monastic robe made of pearls, and gold lamps from the Ming Dynasty. As for the murals, those on the northern side of the corridor on the second floor are the best.

All Buddhist sects consider the Jokhang to be a sacred place. During the first month of the Tibetan lunar calendar in 1409, the Buddhist master Tsongkhapa held the exceptional Mönlam Chenmo or Great Prayer Festival at the Jokhang Temple. Tibetan history acknowledges this grand meeting as the official origin of the Gelugpa or Yellow Hat sect. It then became a tradition to hold the festival annually. In addition, the ceremony to grant the title of Lharampa was performed in the Jokhang's front court. A Lharampa has the Lharam Geshe degree, the highest-ranking of the various *geshe* degrees.

Ramoche Temple (Lhasa)

The Ramoche Temple is in the north of the city of Lhasa and about a kilometer from the Jokhang Temple. It is a key cultural site protected by the Tibet Autonomous Region's government. The Ramoche Temple is one of the oldest religious buildings in Lhasa. It was first built by Princess Wencheng in the seventh century to house the Jowo Sakyamuni statue that she took to Tibet. It was originally built in a Han Chinese style but was rebuilt in a Tibetan style after repeated damage by fire. It was used as the main assembly hall for the Gyuto Tantric University.

The Ramoche Temple faces east and was so built because Princess Wencheng was homesick. It now has an area of about 2,100 square meters and is three stories high. The assembly hall on the ground floor is 21.4 meters long from east to west and 17.6 meters long from north to south. This hall contains the statue of the Buddha Akshobhya brought to Tibet by the Nepalese Princess Bhrikuti Devi (Tritsun), as well as statues of Dipamkara (the Buddha of Fixed Light) and Maitreya. Behind the assembly hall is a rectangular hall for worshiping Buddha that is 4.4 meters long and 5.1 meters wide. A circumambulation route surrounds this hall. On the temple's second story are the monks' quarters and a Buddhist hall with six pillars. On the third floor is a magnificent gilded hall, around which is a circumambulation route. There is also a bedroom preserved for the Dalai Lama's use during his visits to Ramoche.

The Ramoche Temple is one of the oldest religious buildings in Lhasa. It is also regarded as a highly sacred place by all traditions of Tibetan Buddhism. In 1474, the Ramoche Temple was taken over by Kunga Dondrup, a second-generation disciple of Tsongkhapa, and it was used as the main assembly hall for the newly founded Gyuto Tantric University of Ganden Monastery. It has been one of the Gelugpa sect's bases ever since. During the time of the fifth Dalai Lama (1617-82), the Gelugpa sect renovated the Ramoche Temple. In the second month of the Tibetan calendar every year since 1694, a religious assembly called the Tsochod prayer meeting has been held in memory of the fifth Dalai Lama at the Ramoche Temple.

Trandruk Temple (Nedong County, Shannan)

Trandruk Temple is on the eastern bank of the Yarlung River on the route between Tsethang and Yumbulagang. Trandruk is considered to be one of the earliest Buddhist temples built in Tibet. Like the Jokhang and Ramoche temples in Lhasa, its founding is attributed to the seventh-century king Songtsen Gampo. According to tradition, Princess Wencheng perceived the form of a female demon in Tibet's landscape and, to subdue the demon, had the idea of building temples on the most prominent parts of the demon's body. The Jokhang was built on the site of what Wencheng thought was the demon's heart. Four other temples in Tibet are called the Tadul or "extremity-subduing" temples. These are located at places that are said to correspond to the shoulders and hips of the demon. Trandruk Temple is one of the four. During the Tubo Dynasty, Trandruk Temple

was the political center of
Lhoka (Shannan). During
the Pagmotrupa regime,
the temple was repaired
and enlarged by the Ta
Situ, Changchub Gy-
altsen. It was repaired later
on by the fourth Panchen
Lama and the seventh
Dalai Lama.

Trandruk Temple is
situated in the middle of a
village among a cluster of
houses owned by ordinary

Buddha statues in Trandruk Temple's assembly hall.

people. To the right of the main gate going into the monastery, there is a
large bronze bell hanging from a porch. The bell is quite similar to that of
Samye Mo-nastery, and their inscriptions are also similar. The Trandruk
inscription says the bell was made under the supervision of an ethnic Han
bhiksu (religious mendicant) and that the donor, called Jamchub Tsun,
was the third wife of Trisong Detsen. The casting of this bell and of that in
Samye Monastery show that smelting in Tubo between the seventh and
ninth centuries had reached a high skill level and that there were frequent
exchanges between Han and Tibetan people in the area of handicrafts.

Songtsen Gampo is said to have built the temple to house a spontaneously formed image of the bodhisattva Tara that miraculously appeared on
the site. The temple's biggest building is the assembly hall. There are more
than a dozen prayer halls in the temple. The most precious item now in
Trandruk Temple is a *tangka* painting of Tara made in the Yuan Dynasty and
embroidered with 3,000 pearls and jewels.

Tsangdram Lhakhang

The Tsangdram Lhakhang temple, also called Jamtrin Gegye Gompa, is in Pangshing township, Gyirong District, Gyirong County, in Shigatse Prefecture. According to tradition, it was built during the reign of Songtsen Gampo. It is one of the four "extremity-subduing" temples built to suppress a female demon at the time the Jokhang Temple was built.

The main building is a four-story square wooden pavilion-like structure and is about 16 meters high. The ground floor is 22 meters at its widest. The building is hollow inside. Staircases connect each successive story. Tsangdram Lhakhang is now dilapidated but its old architectural style and the Nepalese-style murals are of great significance and worthy of study.

Pabongka (Lhasa)

Pabongka is situated on a big rock in the Nyangtran Gully in Lhasa's northern suburbs, about 10 kilometers west of Sera Monastery. According to tradition, the square cave beneath the rock served as a place for meditation during Songtsen Gampo's reign before the Jokhang and Ramoche temples were built. Statues of Buddha and a shrine for Songtsen Gampo were later set up in the cave.

Songtsen Gampo built a nine-story castle called Maru Palace on the rock. It was made of bricks and stones, with liquid copper filling the cracks, and the castle was strengthened by four big iron chains. After the castle was built, Songtsen Gampo stayed there often, discussing official matters and receiving visitors. It became an important location for political activities. Tradition has it that it was here that Thonmi Sambhota offered Songtsen Gampo his newly created Tibetan script and carved the six syllables of the Lamaist mantra "Om mani padme hum" on the stone wall in front of the Risum Lhakhang Hall, an inscription that is still discernible even today. It was here that Thonmi Sambhota translated 21 exoteric and esoteric Buddhist scriptures from Sanskrit into Tibetan. Songtsen Gampo himself later went on a four-year secluded retreat here to study the newly created Tibetan script. The very first seven Tibetan monks also stayed here after being ordained during Trisong Detsen's reign in the last quarter of the eighth century. It was an important site for Buddhist activities during the Tubo regime. The castle was destroyed during Lang Darma's persecution of Buddhism.

During the second expansion of Buddhism, Kadampa Potowa had his disciples build a two-story temple here and set up a *sangha* (monastic community) to preach Buddhist doctrine. Having been invited to meet Godan Khan, Sakya Pandita Kunga Gyaltsen came here to perform a pilgrimage en route to Liangzhou (now Wuwei in Gansu Province). He preached here and his nephew Phagpa was ordained here. Tsongkhapa also meditated here. Tsongkhapa's disciples built 108 stupas in the western part of the cave, in each stupa preserving a bead from the prayer beads that Tsongkhapa had used. The site later came under the management of Sera Monastery and was the seat of Pabongka Rinpoche, the powerful lama of the Gelugpa sect. It has always been sacred and famous for its scenery and historical relics.

Samye Monastery (Dranang County, Shannan Prefecture)

Samye Monastery is on the north bank of the Yarlung Zangbo River in Dranang County, Shannan Prefecture. It is located at the foot of Hepori, one of Tibet's four sacred mountains. In ancient times, King Trisong Detsen was supposed to have had his palace on this mountain. Samye was founded during the second half of the eighth century under Trisong Detsen's patronage, with the work being directed by Padmasambhava and Shantarakshita, the two Indian masters that the king had invited to Tibet to help preach the Buddhist faith. There are several versions of how the name Samye originated. One version says the name means "monastery beyond people's imagination" and that the monastery was so-called because of its huge scale. Another version says that the three stories of the main building differ from each other in style – the ground floor is in a Tubo style, the second floor Chinese, and the third floor Indian – so the monastery was called Sanyang Monastery (meaning "Three-Styles Monastery") and this name was later mispronounced as Samye.

In fact, Samye Monastery comprises a whole group of buildings. Around the assembly hall are 108 temple halls of all sizes. The monastery's first abbot was the eminent Indian monk Shantarakshita. The main building is the central temple, which represents Mount Sumeru, the mythical mountain at the center of the Buddhist cosmos. Around the central temple are four more temples, which represent the four continents situated in the vast ocean to the north, south, east and west of Sumeru. To the right and left of each of these temples are two smaller temples, representing the subcontinents of the Buddhist universe. Four great stupas in four colors (white, red, blue and green) stand facing the main temple's southeast, southwest, northwest and northeast corners respectively. To the left of the entrance is an ancient stele, which is the record of an edict issued by Trisong Detsen. The ancient Tibetan writing on the front of the tablet is still discernible. An old bell hangs from the roof right above the entrance and might also date back to the times of the early kings. Two attractive stone lions also stand by the entrance. On the door lintel hangs a dark green panel bestowed by a Qing Dynasty emperor with carved Chinese characters painted in gold that read "Gelugpa Monastery. " There are Buddha statues in all the temple halls, and the walls are decorated with murals. The monastery has been repeatedly damaged by fire and then restored but its original style still remains.

Samye was Tibet's first Buddhist monastery, so it has preserved time-honored religious festivals and religious dances up to the present time. Religious dances would be performed several times during the first and fifth months of the Tibetan calendar. At festival time, people would wrestle, race horses, practice archery, sing and dance, and so on. Adherents of Buddhism would also take the opportunity to pay homage to Drakmar, the nearby birthplace of the Tubo *tsenpo* Trisong Detsen, and the renowned retreat of Chimpuk, which is a warren of caves dating back to very early times. Both Padmasambhava and Yeshe Tsogyel lived in Chimpuk for extended periods.

Tombs of the Tibetan Kings (Qonggyai County, Shannan Prefecture)

The Tombs of the Tibetan Kings.

The tombs of the ancient Tibetan kings of the 7th to 9th centuries are in the Yarlung Valley in Qonggyai County, Shannan Prefecture. The General Survey Team of the Tibet Administrative Committee of Cultural Relics conducted a survey of the tombs in 1985 and concluded that there are 16 tombs in the area. The site of the burial ground is 2,706 meters long from east to west and 1,407 meters long from south to north, with a total area of 3.8 million square meters. It can be divided into two parts. The eastern part contains six tombs located at the end of the Dongkar Gully, while the western part contains 10 tombs located in the Mura Valley. The two parts are about 800 meters apart. Nine tombs have been reliably identified as belonging to the following Tubo *tsenpos*: Songtsen Gampo, Mangsong Mangtsen, Tride Songtsen, Trisong Detsen, Tritsug Detsen, Tride Tsugtsen, Lang Darma, Tri Dusong Mangpoje, and Muni Tsenpo.

Most of the tombs are at the foot of a hill and have a square or trapezoid-shaped floor plan. The biggest tomb is 180 meters long and 14.7 meters wide and looks like a hill. The tombs were made of soil, stone, timber and grass. Every layer was rammed together and a pile of timber was inserted between the layers filled with rammed earth.

The central chamber contains the graves of Songtsen Gampo and his two wives, Princess Wencheng and Princess Bhrikuti Devi (Tritsun). On each of the four sides is a side chamber connected to the central chamber by a tomb passage. The burial accessories include a great amount of weaponry, jewelry, gold vessels, silverware and household goods used by Songtsen Gampo before his death.

At the southern end of the western section is the tomb of the *tsenpo* Trisong Detsen. In front of the tomb are two fine stone carved lions in the Tang style. At the northeast corner of the tomb is a stone stele. The ancient Tibetan writing on the front of the tablet records Trisong Detsen's achievements and is still decipherable. Vivid decorative patterns are carved on the top of the tablet, and there is an upright flying dragon on each of the tablet's sides.

The Tubo kings' tombs are magnificent, impressive and majestic in structure. The impact of Buddhism meant that no more tombs were built after the Tubo Dynasty collapsed. Therefore, the kings' tombs in Qonggyai are of great importance because they are the only tomb buildings in Tibet and occupy an important position in architectural history.

The Tombs of the Tibetan Kings.

Dunhuang Sutra Cave and Tubo Murals

The Sutra Cave is the 17th cave in the Mogao Grottoes and was discovered in 1900. It is a cave cut in the wall in the 16th cave's passage. It is a meter above the ground and is 25 meters long, 27 meters wide, and three meters high. In addition to murals and statues, handwritten sutras and documents have been discovered in the cave. In total, there were about 50,000 items, including handwritten sutras, documents, embroidery, pictures, religious implements and other cultural relics.

The historical documents discovered at Dunhuang were written not only in Chinese but also in the Tibetan, Sanskrit, Hotan, Sogdian, Tocharian and ancient Uygur (Huihu) languages. Of the historical Tibetan documents, London and Paris are home to roughly 2,000 items each, while there are more than 400 items in Beijing Library, and about 10,000 items in Gansu Province and elsewhere. A few items are in Russia and Japan. These ancient Tibetan documents are of great significance for the study of Tibetan history, religion and culture.

The so-called Tubo murals in Dunhuang refer to the murals in the Mogao Grottoes and in the Yulin Grottoes in Gansu's Anxi County between 781 and 848 when the Tubo occupied Dunhuang. Forty-four of the Dunhuang Mogao Grottoes were first opened during the Tubo period. Of these, the best are considered to be the murals in the caves numbered 112, 158, 159, 231, 237, 359, 360 and 361.

The Tubo murals in Dunhuang occupy a very important position in the development of the Dunhuang murals. They are a link between the murals produced when the Tang Dynasty was at its height and those produced during the late Tang Dynasty.

Tang-Tubo Alliance Tablet (Lhasa)

The Tang-Tubo alliance tablet was erected in 823 in front of the Jokhang Temple in Lhasa, under the Jowo Utra or Buddha's Hair (a large willow tree planted by Princess Wencheng). In 821, the Tubo sent a mission to Chang'an to appeal for a mutual pledge of peace. This is known historically as the Changqing Alliance (the Tang Dynasty's Changqing period covering the years from 821 to 824) or the Uncle-Nephew Alliance. In 822, the Tang court dispatched a mission to Rasa (Lhasa) to attend a ceremony to pledge peace. To express their sincerity about peace and friendship, the Tang erected a tablet in Chang'an while the Tubo erected this tablet in Lhasa.

The Lhasa tablet still stands near the Jokhang Temple entrance. It is 4.78 meters high, 95 centimeters wide and 50 centimeters thick. It bears an inscription in both Tibetan and Chinese. The inscription recounts the close ties between the two sides and expresses their common wish for lasting peace. Both sides of the tablet have a carved list of the names of those who took part in the alliance conference, comprising 18 Tang court officials and 17 Tubo officials. The tablet is a very important cultural relic for the study of Tubo official posts, clans, language, and relations between the Tang and Tubo. It pro-

The Tang-Tubo Alliance Tablet.

vides ironclad evidence of the mille-nium-old friendly relationship between the Han and Tibetan peoples.

Rock Carvings on Chakpori Hill (Lhasa)

Chakpori Hill (called Yaowang Shan in Chinese, meaning Hill of the King of Medicine) is at the southwest of the Potala Palace in Lhasa. It was first opened up during the Tubo period, and the number of rock carvings increased over time. Thousands of rock carvings now cover the hill for about

Cliff paintings on Chakpori Hill (Yaowang Shan).

two kilometers. The smallest carving is less than a foot (30 centimeters) high, while the biggest is several meters high. The carvings consist of Buddhist images, including images of Buddhas, bodhisattvas, tantric deities, protector deities, devas and eminent Tibetan monks of the past, as well as the six-syllable Lamaist mantra "Om mani padme hum." Most of the carvings were done by folk artists, and many good works are among them.

Chingwa Taktse Castle and the Cliff Carvings on Mount Chingwa Taktse

Chingwa Taktse Castle is on Mount Chingwa Taktse in Qonggyai Country, Shannan Prefecture. It was built on this cliff top early in the Tubo Dynasty. According to Tibetan records, the castle was originally built by the Tubo king Pude Gungyal. Early in the Tubo Dynasty, the Qonggyai area of the Yarlung Valley was a center of Tubo activity, and their king lived in this castle. Its ruins are still clearly visible on the cliff.

Cliff paintings on Chakpori Hill (Yaowang Shan).

The carvings on Mount Chingwa Taktse are in two separate areas on the cliff. The dates of the carvings are unknown. There are 56 images of Buddhas, bodhisattvas and protector deities. The biggest carving is about 3 meters high and the smallest is 15 centimeters high. There are also carvings of the six-syllable Lamaist mantra "Om mani padme hum."

Chapter 3

Sites of Guge Kingdom Relics

A Period of Separatist Regimes and the Revival of Buddhism in Tibet

After the Tubo Dynasty collapsed, the Qinghai-Tibet Plateau did not have a centralized regime during the 370 years from 869 to 1239. This period of Tibetan history was one of political division under inde-

A *tangka* showing Yumtan and Osung.

pendent regimes. During this time, Yumtan, Lang Darma's adopted son, occupied Lhasa and the Samye area. Osung, Lang Darma's second son, seized Lhoka (today's Shannan area). In 905, Osung was killed when his ministers poisoned him in Yarlung. After Osung's death, his son Palkhor Tsen fled to Shigatse in the Tsang region, where he built castles and settled his vassals. In 923, Palkhor Tsen was killed by insurrectionary troops. After that, his elder son Tashi Tsekpapal ruled in Gyangzê in Tsang, and the younger son Kyide Nyimagon fled to Burang in the Ngari region, where he married the daughter of a local aristocrat. Kyide Nyimagon's three sons occupied Ladakh, Burang and Guge. They later established the Ladakh and Guge kingdoms.

After the fall of Tang Dynasty, the Tibetan tribal chieftains of the Hehuang region (covering the Yellow and Huang Shui river valleys in present-day eastern Qinghai) made Gyalsra their leader. Of all the separatist Tubo regimes, the most powerful was the Gyalsra regime. The chieftain Gyalsra claimed that he was a descendant of the Tubo *tsenpos*.

Other places on the Qinghai-Tibet Plateau were controlled by independent local chieftains, some of whom were from newly rising families and some of whom were descendants of aristocratic families from the Tubo Dynasty. These chieftains became independent feudal manorial lords. The peasants and herdsmen, including landholding peasants, who emerged after the Tubo Dynasty broke up and the tribal system collapsed, became vassals of the feudal lords because they had been prisoners of war, had gone into debt and become bankrupt, or were seeking the protection of religious-political leaders. Commoners, who had been the main producers during the Tubo Dynasty, gradually became serfs, dependent on manorial lords. The serf system was thus established in all parts of Tibet.

Another characteristic of this period of division was the revival of Buddhism in Tibet. When Lang Darma persecuted and suppressed Buddhism, three monks – named Tsang Rabsal, Yogajung, and Ma Sakyamuni – fled to Qinghai and lived in Dantig Monastery in what is now Hualong County. They took as their disciple a local man called Lachen Gongpa Rabsal. When they were going to ordain him, they invited two ethnic Han monks to take part in the ordination ritual because there were not enough *acharyas* (teachers or masters). A Buddhist center was gradually formed in Hehuang region. In around 936, the local chieftain of the Samye area, Yeshe Gyaltsen (a sixth-generation descendant of Yumtan), sent a 10-man group from Ü-Tsang (central Tibet) headed by Lumed Tsultrim Sherab to Qinghai to study with a disciple of Lachen Gongpa Rabsal. When they returned to Tibet to preach Buddhist doctrine, they had many monasteries built or rebuilt and a number of monastic communities established. Tibetan historians call this development the "propagation of Buddhism from Domed." Lumed set up a monastic community in Lhasa in 949, so Tibetan historians considered this the year of Tibetan Buddhism's revival.

Not long afterward, Yeshe Od, the king of Guge, built several monasteries and sent young men to India to study Buddhist scripture in order to revive Buddhism in Tibet. One of those sent to India was the great translator Rinchen Zangpo, who went to India three times. He later became the abbot of Toling Monastery, translated Buddhist sutras, taught disciples, and gradually spread Buddhism in central Tibet. Tibetan historians call this the "propagation of Buddhism from Ngari."

In the first century of Tibetan Buddhism's revival, the 10 men from Ü-Tsang had many monasteries built and monastic communities organized, forming the mainstream of Tibetan Buddhism. Ewang Monastery and Samada Monastery in Khangmar County, Shalu-Gyalgon Monastery, and Dranang Monastery still exist. Their religious works of art reflect the influence of art from Tibet's Han areas and the Longyou area of Hexi (the area in modern Gansu Province under Tubo occupation). The works are among the best of Tibetan Buddhist art.

The Guge king also invited Atisha, an eminent Bengali monk, to preach in Tibet in 1042. Drom Tonpa (1004-64), a leading Buddhist in Ü-Tsang (central Tibet), invited Atisha to preach there in 1045. After Atisha died in Nyethang in 1054, Drom Tonpa became his successor. In 1056, he built Reting Monastery to the north of Lhasa, from which developed the Kadampa sect.

At that time, Surpoche (1002-62), a Buddhist monk who practiced at home, built Upalung Monastery and collated the scriptures translated during the Tubo Dynasty. The Nyingma sect developed from this monastery.

In 1073, Konchok Gyalpo of the Khon family built Sakya Monastery, from which the Sakya sect developed.

Marpa was one of the greatest Tibetan translators and the founder of the Kagyu school of Tibetan Buddhism. He was also the teacher of the re-nowned Tibetan poet-saint Milarepa. Milarepa's disciple Dakpo Lhaje built Dakpo Monastery in 1121, and Khyungpo Naljorpa built Shangpa Monastery in the same year. The Dakpo Kagyu and Shangpa Kagyu schools of Buddhism developed from these two monasteries.

In the Dakpo Kagyu school, Dusum Khyenpa, a prominent disciple of Dakpo Lhaje, built Karma Monastery in Qamdo in 1147 and Tsurpu Monastery in 1187, from which developed the Karma Kagyu sect. In 1185, Phagmo Drupa, another outstanding disciple, built Dansa Thel Monastery and founded the Pagtru Kagyu sect. In 1160, Darma Wangchuk, yet another prominent disciple, built Barom Monastery and founded the Barom Kagyu sect. In 1175, Shang Tsalpa, also a prominent disciple, built Tsalpa Monastery and founded the Tsalpa Kagyu sect. These are the four major lineages of the Dakpo Kagyu tradition.

In the Pagtru Kagyu school, Phagmo Drupa's disciple Drigungpa Rinchenpal built Drigung Monastery in 1179, from which the Drigung Kagyu sect developed. Taklung Thangpa Tashipal built Taklung Monastery in 1180, from which developed

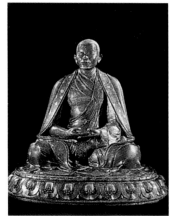

Dusum Khyenpa, founder of the Karma Kagyu sect.

the Taklung Kagyu sect. Lingre Padma Dorje developed the Drukpa Kagyu sect and, in 1193, his disciple Tsangpa Gyare built Druk and Ralung Gompa monasteries. Kalden Yeshe Sengge founded the Yazang Kagyu sect and, in 1206, his disciple Chomonlam built Samye Monastery. Gyaltsa and his brother Kunden built Trophu Monastery and founded the Trophu Kagyu sect. Tsultrim Sengge built Shugseb Monastery in 1181, from which developed the Shugseb Kagyu sect. Yeshe Tsekpa built Yerpa Monastery and founded the Yerpa Kagyu sect; and Sherab Sengge founded the Martsang Kagyu sect. These eight sects are called the "eight minor branches of Dakpo Kagyu." Drukpa Kagyu is also divided into several subbranches: the Middle, Upper, Lower, and Southern Drukpa. The seat of the Southern Drukpa is in Bhutan.

Several features characterized the revival of Tibetan Buddhism:

(1) The lack of a unified political entity meant that independent local regimes ganged up with Buddhist monasteries, so various sects formed. Such a phenomenon did not exist when Buddhism was first propagated in Tibet.

(2) Some monasteries had landholdings and vassals. For instance, the Guge royal house gave some villages (*shika* in Tibetan) to Rinchen Zangpo. This is the earliest record of manors being held by monasteries. The manorial vassals of families who followed the Sakya sect were combined with the monasteries to form the basis of the politico-religious regime.

(3) Tibetan Buddhism during the Tubo Dynasty stressed the worship of the Buddha Sakyamuni but, after the revival of Tibetan Buddhism, a Buddhist was asked to worship his sect's patriarch and to regard his master as a Buddha. The endeavors of Drom Tonpa, Milarepa, Sachen Kunga Nyingpo and so on further localized Buddhism in Tibet.

During the period of division, monks came from Hexi, Longyou

Rituals being performed during a Buddhist assembly.

and India to preach Buddhist doctrine in Tibet, while some eminent Tibetan monks went to preach in Qinghai, Western Xia (Xi Xia) and elsewhere. The Western Xia Dynasty granted some Tibetan monks honorific titles such as Imperial Preceptor and State Preceptor. The economic support the Western Xia gave Tibet played an important role in the development of Buddhism in Tibet. Tibet maintained economic ties with the areas inhabited by Han people throughout the Gyalsra regime and the Western Xia. These ties were clearly demonstrated by the flourishing exchange of Tibetan horses for Han tea during the Song dynasty (960-1279).

Tibet during the period of division was characterized by (1) the existence of a number of independent political regimes each under the control of a local prince or lord and (2) the revival of Tibetan Buddhism. Therefore,

*cultural life at this time was dominated by the monasteries of various reli-
gious sects, including Toling, Nyethang Drolma Lhakhang, Reting, Dansa
Thel, Nartang, Drathang, Karma, and Tselgungtang monasteries. Ruins and
works of art of the renowned Guge kingdom are representative of cultural
relics from this period.*

Toling Monastery (Zanda County, Ngari)

Toling Monastery is on the southern side of the Langchên Zangbo
River in the northwest of Zanda County in Tibet's Ngari region. It was a
well-known monastery in Ngari and was built in the 11th century by the
Guge king Yeshe Od as a place where the great translator Rinchen Zangpo
could preach.

Toling Monastery was originally like Samye Monastery in scale and
form. Now only three halls and a pagoda are in relatively good condition.
Of the three halls, the Nampar Nangzed Lhakhang (All-Knowing
Tathagata Hall) is in the best condition. The hall's layout looks like a
mandala. In the center is a square hall symbolizing Mount Sumeru, to
the sides of which are four groups of shrines symbolizing four
continents. There are also four small pagodas with upturned eaves,
symbolizing the four deva-kings. The hall is 53.5 meters long from east
to west and 48.5 meters long from north to south. It still retains some
characteristics of Buddhist buildings from the Tubo period. Around each
of the three outside halls to the south, north, and west is a circumambulation route. There is another such route around the central hall and
the small halls. This structure is typical of a Tibetan Buddhist monastery from the Tubo period.

Nyethang Drolma Lhakhang

The Nyethang Drolma Lhakhang is on the western side of the Lhasa

River, 20 kilometers southwest of Lhasa itself. In the mid-11th century, Atisha, the Indian Buddhist scholar from the royal family of the small state of Sahor in ancient Bengal, came to Tibet at the invitation of the king of Ngari. He preached first at Toling Monastery. When he was preparing to go back to India, he was invited by Drom Tonpa to preach in the Ü region (eastern central Tibet), and he spread Buddhism in the area around the Lhasa River. Atisha died in Nyethang in 1054. After Atisha's death, Drom Tonpa inherited the monk's teaching role. The next year, Drom Tonpa called all of Atisha's other disciples together to hold a memorial meeting for the anniversary of Atisha's death in Nyethang, where Drom Tonpa built a stupa for Atisha's ashes, 100,000 small *tsa-tsa* (small clay figurines) made with earth and Atisha's ashes, and a statue of Atisha. Then Drom Tonpa and his followers went to a place north of Lhasa called Reting to spread Atisha's teachings. Drom Tonpa built Reting Monastery and founded the Kadampa sect. Not long after, the followers of the Kadampa sect built a temple near the Atisha stupa. In the temple was a bronze statue of White Tara, Atisha's personal tutelary tantric deity. The temple was therefore called Drolma Lhakhang (Temple of Tara). It was a holy site worshipped by monks and lay followers of the Kadampa and Gelugpa sects. During the 1920s, Reting Rinpoche, who was then the regent of Tibet, had the temple rebuilt and enlarged.

The Drolma Lhakhang is a two-story building. In the central hall on the ground floor is a silver statue of White Tara; in the eastern hall, there is an image of Atisha and a statue of Tara; and in the western hall, there is a stupa of a victorious Vijaya and a bronze stupa said to have been built by Ashoka. The upper floor consists of a chapel, in which previous Dalai Lamas and eminent monks held Buddhist activities when they were attending the winter sutra debates at Dewachen Monastery, 15 kilometers northwest of Nyethang.

Reting Monastery (Lhunzhub County, Lhasa Municipality)

Reting Monastery was the Kadampa sect's first monastery and is in the north of Lhunzhub County. Drom Tonpa built it in 1057. Its main building faces south. The ground floor consists of a large assembly hall, surrounding which are several small prayer halls with Buddha images and Buddhist sutras inside. Inside the prayer halls, the walls are lined with sutra cases, while the outer walls are made of stone. On the floor above are several bedrooms for the Dalai Lama and regent to stay when they passed by on an inspection tour. There are also several *lhakhangs* (temples) and storerooms on this floor. Unlike other monasteries of the Gelugpa (Yellow Hat sect), Reting Monastery does not have a *dratsang* (college) or *khangtsen* (community of student monks). The regent Reting Rinpoche (reincarnate lama) held politico-religious power. The lineage of abbots was passed from tutor to disciple. The Reting incarnation system began in the 16th century when the monastery ceased to be a Kadampa monastery and was taken over by the Gelugpa order. Originally the monastery had only about 50 monks. Then it developed into a large monastery with 500 monks, 33 manors, seven subsidiary monasteries, and three pasture areas.

The monastery's traditional religious festivals are the Dance of the Dorje God held on the 15th day of the first month of the Tibetan calendar, the Festival of the Cuckoo Worshipping the Buddha on the 15th day of the fourth lunar month; the Festival of Worshipping the Buddha with Flowers on the 15th day of the seventh month; and the festivals Papongtangko and Circumambulating the Spirits' Chime Stone on the 15th day of the seventh month during the year of the goat in the Tibetan calendar. When the Papongtangko festival resumed in 1991, tens of thousands of people came to the monastery, making the day an exceptionally grand occasion.

Dansa Thel Monastery (Sangri County, Shannan)

Dansa Thel was the first monastery of the Pagtru Kagyu sect. It is in what is now Sangri County in southern Tibet. Dorje Gyalpo, a Kagyupa monk, went to a place then called Pagmotru in 1158. He built a small monastery there and preached in it for more than 10 years until he died. Dorje Gyalpo was known as Phagmotrupa, and the religious sect he founded was called Phagmotrupa. The monastery later became the renowned Dansa Thel Monastery.

In 1208, Drakpa Jungne (1175-1255), a monk from a local rich family called Lang, became the monastery's abbot. Members of the Lang family have since held the post of abbot, generation after generation. The rulers of the Yuan Dynasty (1271-1368) granted 13 local regimes in Ü-Tsang the title of *trikor* (an early administrative unit that was theoretically a myriarchy or a unit comprising 10,000 households). Pagtru was one of the regimes made a

Young monks.

trikor. The abbot of Dansa Thel was responsible for nominating the chieftain of the Pagtru *trikor*.

In the 1320s, Changchub Gyaltsen, a descendant of Drakpa Jungne, was the Pagtru *trikor* chieftain. He had religious and political power in his hands, seized the greater part of Ü by military force, and battled with the Sakya sect. He established the Pagtru Desi regime. In 1351, he built Tsethang Monastery, which took over the important role played by Dansa Thel.

Ancient Kingdom of Guge and Its Ruins

The site of the Guge kingdom.

The Guge kingdom was in Shangshung, a place of an ancient mysterious civilization. Its capital was at the modern Zanda County of Ngari. In the early decades of the 10th century, owing to the uprisings of slaves and commoners and the division of the Tubo royal house caused by the struggle for power, Kyide Nyimagon, a descendant of Tubo royal family, was forced to flee to the western Ngari, where he founded a new regime. He had three sons, who each established an independent kingdom: the Guge, Ladakh, and Burang kingdoms. The Guge kingdom was important in Tibetan history. It was a strong local regime in the period of division after the fall of the Tubo Dynasty and was also the cradle of the "propagation of Buddhism from Ngari" during the revival of Tibetan Buddhism. Its royal lineage continued until the 15th century.

The site of the Guge kingdom was one of China's first cultural heritage sites to be given state protection. In Tsaparang by the bank of the Langchên Zangbo River, within the territory of the present-day Zanda County in Ngari Prefecture, there is a mound of yellow earth about 300 meters high. On the hill lie the ruins of a wall and a castle, the most important remains of the ancient Guge kingdom. The ruins occupy an area of 180,000 square meters and consist of about 300 houses, 300 caves, and three pagodas each about 10 meters high. Together, these form a magnificent cluster of temple buildings, preserved intact. A fortification wall surrounds the entire complex, with four earthen forts standing at the wall's four corners. There are four temples and two halls, in which there are many lifelike murals and statues. There are also the remains of many pieces of armor, shields and arrows. Inside the building complex, tunnels of a total length of about 2 kilometers run in all directions.

Numerous cultural relics have been found in the Guge ruins but there are only a few bronze items made in the 11th and 12th centuries. Most of the relics are small gold and bronze statues in Indian Pala or Kashmiri styles. These statues are simple in style, stressing muscles and spiritual power. Statues from the 13th and 14th centuries were exquisitely made, the figures wearing high hair knots and hats. The gold and bronze statues excavated from the castle may serve as examples of this. After the 15th century, statues were characterized by their large size. By absorbing the Kashmiri, Indian-Nepalese, and Ü-Tsang styles, Guge sculpture developed its own unique style. The statue of the meditating Buddha in the Red Temple is from an early date. The elegantly made image has a proportional build, with long limbs, an oval face, and gentle eyes. The smile is mysterious and kind. The large statue of the sitting Buddha in the White Temple is a representative 16th-century work. The proportions are bigger and the figure is beautifully dressed. The Buddha's calm and solemn appearance displays the demeanor of future life. The beautiful decorations of the halo and throne make this image of Buddha brilliant.

The paintings from the Guge site are better preserved. Most of them are magnificent murals. A few *tangkas* were lost by being taken abroad. The Guge site has many "courtyard paintings" of a luxurious and complicated style. Such a large number of excellent pictures with such rich content cannot be found anywhere else in Tibet.

Nartang Monastery (Shigatse)

Twenty kilometers southwest of Shigatse is Nartang Monastery, which was founded in 1033 by the Kadampa sect monk Tumton Lodro Drakpa. In Tibetan, *nar* means "nose," and *tang* means "flat ground" but the monastery was also called the Elephant-Trunk Flat-Land Monastery. Many eminent monks preached in the monastery. The first Dalai Lama, Gedun Druppa, was ordained in this monastery and studied Buddhist doctrine there for 17 years.

Nartang Monastery has a great hall and 13 prayer halls dedicated to Maitreya, Sakyamuni and others. To the side of the great hall is a temple that houses stupas of the monastery's successive *tulkus* (incarnate lamas). Formerly the monastery had precious *tangka* paintings of the Ming and Qing dynasties and a tablet with the Chinese characters "Shan En Si" (Virtuous Grace Monastery) written by the Qing Emperor Yongzheng (reigned 1722-35). The monastery was renowned for its sutra printing house.

To salvage and develop ancient Tibetan books and Buddhist sutras, the local government of the time founded a large sutra printing house in 1730. It took more than 20 years and a large amount of money to build. When the printing house was established, it recruited renowned calligraphers, sculptors and painters from all parts of Tibet and brought together a group of prominent young men to learn woodblock printing. Over time, the monastery's printing house printed many great Tibetan Buddhist works, such as the *Kangyur* ("Translation of the Word," discourses attributed to Sakyamuni) in 108 volumes, the *Tengyur* ("Transmitted Word," commentaries on the discourses) in 215 volumes, and a biography of Sakyamuni. The Nartang edition of the entire Buddhist canon was distributed far and wide and had a great influence in Tibetan areas. The monastery is not as large as it once was, and the printing house is no longer there, yet the piles of wooden printing blocks there show how big the printing house was.

Drathang Monastery (Shannan)

Drathang Monastery was built in 1081 by the Kadampa sect monk Drapa Ngonshe. The monastery is in the suburbs of Dranang County in Shannan Prefecture. It is surrounded by three walls. The outside wall is circular, while the middle and innermost walls are multisided. The main hall faces east and originally had three stories but now has one. Murals cover all of the walls of the main hall. The style indicates that they were painted when the monastery was built. The murals are of great value for the study of Tibetan art history.

Chapter 4

Sakya Monastery

Tibet's Incorporation into Chinese Territory and its Continuous Development

In the late 12th and early 13th century, the Mongols in north China rose rapidly. In 1206, the Mongol tribal chieftain Genghis Khan annexed all the other Mongol tribes and established a Mongol khanate. He later founded a new dynasty by unifying the whole of China and all of its ethic groups. During these great historical changes, one after another of the Tibetan-inhabited areas joined the waves of unification as a result of the economic, cultural and political exchanges between Tibetan areas on the one hand and China's hinterland and northern pasture lands on the other.

While conquering the Western Xia and embarking on an expedition west into central Asia, the Mongol royal family came into contact with Tibetans and Tibetan Buddhism. In 1239, the Mongol prince Godan sent a military expedition under the command of General Dorta Nagpo from Gansu and Qinghai into Tibet. Because the Tibetan religious sects were independent from each other and the tribal leagues could not effectively resist the Mongol invasion, the Mongol army very soon moved north of Lhasa to take control of the main areas of Tibet, where it established post stations for matériel support. Then Dorta Nagpo tried to make contact with influential Tibetan Buddhists. He was very well familiar with the various Tibetan Buddhist sects. He first invited the most influential Buddhist leader in the Ü region, the Drigung Kagyu sect's Chen-nga Rinpoche Drakpa Jungne (1175-1255), to meet Godan in a Mongol area. This attempt failed but helped bring about the historic meeting between Sakya Pandita Kunga Gyaltsen and Godan in Liangzhou.

Sakya Pandita Kunga Gyaltsen (1182-1251) was the fourth of the five patriarchs of the Sakya sect. As a boy, he was ordained a monk by his uncle Drakpa Gyaltsen. Then he studied under Kache Panchen Shakya Shri, an eminent Kashmiri monk who went to Tibet in 1204. As an eminent Tibetan Buddhist master, Kunga Gyaltsen had a good command of the five greater and five lesser sciences of ancient India, wrote many books, preached widely in Ü-Tsang, had many disciples, and was experienced in political and religious affairs. The Sakya sect that he led was the most influential sect in Tsang. He accepted the Mongol leader Godan's invitation and promised to go to Liangzhou. Before setting off, he arranged all the affairs of the Sakya sect well. It seemed that he had considered what might happen after he had gone to Liangzhou. To successfully pass on his post to his nephew Phagpa in accordance with tradition, Kunga Gyaltsen decided to go with his two nephews, Phagpa and his brother Chakna Dorje, to Liangzhou. Kunga Gyaltsen held talks with lay and religious leaders along the way, explaining why he promised to go to meet the Mongol leader. He said it was for Buddhism and all the people. At Drakpa Jungne's invitation, Kunga Gyaltsen went to Drigung Monastery to meet him and accepted his gifts. This showed that Kunga Gyaltsen's trip to Liangzhou was not to establish a personal relationship with the Mongols. Instead, he went to Liangzhou on behalf of Tibet's lay and religious leaders, including Drakpa Jungne, to hold peace talks with Godan.

The Sakya Pandita.

After a journey of about two years, Kunga Gyaltsen and his party reached Liangzhou in August 1246. He held talks with Godan at the beginning of 1247 regarding Tibet's submission to Mongolia. The terms were that Tibet's lay and religious leaders should give allegiance and pay tribute to the Mongols and pledge to be Mongol subjects under Mongol control and that the Mongols would leave intact the Tibetan leaders' original posts and power and let them have the corresponding official positions. Having come to terms with Godan, Kunga Gyaltsen in his capacity as a Tibetan Buddhist leader passed on the terms to Tibet's lay and religious leaders, advising them to accept the terms. He sent letters from Liangzhou to Tibetan secular and monastic leaders. He told them that, in the long-term interests of Buddhism and the Tibetan people, they should give up any intention of military resistance and instead submit to the Mongols according to the terms he had reached. Sakya Pandita Kunga Gyaltsen's letter to the Tibetans is quite well known, and the full text of it appeared in *Sakya's Lineal Description*.

Kunga Gyaltsen died by the end of 1251 in Liangzhou. On his deathbed, he handed his cassock and alms bowl to Phagpa and entrusted all his other disciples to Phagpa. Thus Phagpa became the fifth hierarch of the Sakya sect. Phagpa was 17 years old at the time and he immediately carried out his political and religious duties. In 1251, Monge Khan ascended the throne.

To grant land to the other Mongol princes and thus harmonize relations with them, he ordered that a new census be carried out in all places under Mongol control, including Tibet. Each of his brothers was then granted part of Tibet. Monge Khan received Drigung in Ü and Chumik in Tsang. Kublai received Tsalpa in Ü, Hulagu got Pagtru and Yazang in Ü, Alibugo got Taklung in Ü, and Godan got Sakya. Each prince made contact with the influential sect of the area granted to him, and treated its leader as his religious tutor. The Drigung, Pagtru, and Tsalpa *trikors* (myriarchies) were established at that time.

In 1252, Kublai sent an envoy to invite both Sakya Pandita Kunga Gyaltsen, who had been in Liangzhou, and Karma Pakshi, who was then in Kham, to attend an audience with him in the Liupan Mountains. Since Kunga Gyaltsen had already died, Phagpa was invited to meet Kublai and the two began to have close relations after their meeting. Phagpa initiated Kublai into the Hevajra tantra at New Year in 1253. *Sakya's Lineal Description* says that Kublai, in return for the initiation, gave Phagpa a precious jade seal, a cassock decorated with pearls, a canopy, a golden saddle, and horses as gifts. Phagpa thus became Kublai's adviser and assistant in religious affairs and followed Kublai to live in the city of Kaiping (the then capital city of the Mongol khanate and now Duolun or Dolonnur County in Inner Mongolia).

In 1259, Monge Khan was killed in a military expedition against the Southern Song Dynasty in Sichuan. In March the next year, Kublai succeeded Monge as Great Khan at Kaiping with the sup-

A jade statue of Phagpa.

port of the princes and ministers. His ascension to the throne symbolized the Mongolian khanate's change into a new Chinese dynasty, the Yuan Dynasty. In the late 1260s, Kublai granted Phagpa the title of state preceptor as well as a jade seal of authority. Kublai put Phagpa in charge of Buddhist affairs throughout the entire nation. In 1264, Kublai sent Phagpa and Phagpa's brother Chakna Dorje to go from the capital city back to Tibet. On the eve of their departure, Kublai granted Phagpa a special imperial edict (the Pearl Edict) and granted Chakna Dorje the title of Prince Palen, as well as a gold seal of authority. This bestowal meant that Kublai had entrusted the brothers with the local administration of Tibet.

At that time, the Supreme Control Commission in Charge of all Buddhist Monks (Zongzhi Yuan or General Council) was established as a central government department to manage Buddhist affairs in the entire nation and also the local administration of Tibet. It was renamed the Commission for Buddhist and Tibetan Affairs (Xuanzheng Yuan or Political Council) in 1288. Kublai put Phagpa in control of the General Council. Under the State Preceptor Phagpa, there was a commissioner responsible for the day-to-day running of the commission. Under the commissioner were a *tongzhi* (associate administrator), a *fushi* (deputy director) and a *qianyuan* (deputy commissioner).

Originally there were two commissioners on the Political Council. The number later ranged from one to six or 10. A commissioner had the power to appoint and remove his subordinates. Among his officials were laymen and monks, as well as Mongolian aristocrats and Tibetan people. It is well known that Kublai's minister Senge was a Tibetan appointed as a Political Council commissioner. As important officials of the Yuan court, the commissioners were appointed directly by the emperor. This demonstrates that the administrative system established by Phagpa was, from the beginning, part of the Yuan Dynasty's system of administration. Phagpa was not only in charge of Buddhist affairs throughout the whole nation and, in particular, of all the sects and monasteries of Tibetan Buddhism but also had the Political Council under his jurisdiction. This showed that the administrative system designed for Tibet by Kublai and Phagpa was a politico-religious system.

The high officials of Tibetan administrative institutions were nominated by the state preceptor or the Political Council, and the nomination had to be submitted to the imperial court for the emperor's approval. The emperor would bestow gold or silver tablets, seals, and certificates of appointment on the appointed officials. According to Tibetan and Chinese historical records, the Tibetan officials, who had aristocratic or monastic backgrounds, were mostly nominated by the state preceptor, while pacification commissioners, chief military commanders, and *darkhaches* (seal-holding officials) were nominated by the Political Council. The council was also responsible for implementing the law in Tibet, carrying out population censuses, making peace between *trikors*, arbitrating in lawsuits, and helping the Bureau of Military Affairs to carry out military activities in Tibet.

After going back to Tibet in 1265, Phagpa divided the various local politico-religious regimes into myriarchies according to the size of their forces and territory. He appointed the heads of the local politico-religious regimes as leaders of the myriarchies. These administrative units were under the jurisdiction of the Sakya regime, whose supreme leader was Phagpa. Phagpa went once

A gilded iron tablet bestowed on the Sakya ruling lama by the Yuan emperor. The engraving in the Pakpa script says: "This is the emperor's order. Those who disobey the order should be punished."

more to the Yuan capital Dadu (modern Beijing) in 1269 to offer Kublai a new alphabetic writing system for the Mongolian language, which had been created by order of the emperor. Kublai bestowed on Phagpa the honorific title of Imperial Preceptor. The post of Imperial Preceptor then

A jade seal of authority bestowed by the Yuan emperor on the Sakya ruling lama.

remained in existence for the whole duration of the Yuan Dynasty and was usually held by a member of the Sakya Khon family. If the family had no qualified person to assume the post, a high-ranking monk of the Sakya sect would take the post. When the Imperial Preceptor was staying in Dadu, the abbot of Sakya Monastery (the Sakya ruling lama) would be in charge of the Sakya regime. Since the Imperial Preceptor and the Sakya ruling lama were both monks, a Sakya *ponchen* (a high official under the Imperial Preceptor and Sakya ruling lama) was appointed to take charge of administrative affairs. A *langchen* was appointed to manage the subjects within the Sakya regime's jurisdiction. Phagpa established for himself a *labrang* or *lhadrang* (dynastic house), consisting of a group of his attendants. The leaders of many other Buddhist sects then followed suit by setting up their own dynastic house, which became required personal offices for leaders who held politico-religious power.

In about 1280, after the conflicts in the Sakya ruling clique had been resolved and Phagpa had died, the Yuan Dynasty established the Ü-Tsang Pacification Commission. In 1292, after the rebellion of the Drigung sect against the Sakya sect had been quashed, in accordance with a proposal by the Political Council, Kublai combined the Ü-Tsang Pacification Commission and the Ngari region's chief military commander into the Pacification Commission and Chief Military Command for the Three Circuits of Ü-Tsang and Ngari Korsum. The commission was responsible for passing on the central government's orders, administering post stations, and controlling the troops stationed in Tibet. Tibetan historical records say that some Sakya *ponchens* had been officials of the Yuan central government's Political Council and that some *ponchens* were concurrently pacification commissioners of Ü-Tsang. The Yuan Dynasty sent officials to Tibet several times to carry out a census with the help of the Sakya *ponchen*, determine the amount that a myriarchy should pay in tribute and taxes, set up post stations, and establish the *wula* corvée system to guarantee the smooth running of post-station transportation. These measures made it possible for the Yuan Dynasty to station troops, set up government offices at various levels, and enforce its policies and orders in Tibet.

After Phagpa's death, there was a power struggle within the Sakya Khon family, which had dominant control of Tibet with the support of the Yuan Dynasty. Phagpa's nephew Dharmapala, who succeeded Phagpa as Imperial Preceptor, declared that his cousin Danyi Chenpo Zangpo Pal was not an authentic descendant of the Khon family. Kublai exiled Zangpo Pal to Hangzhou, south of the Yangtze River. After Dharmapala died, the family had no successor. The Yuan

A seal and inscription given to Prince Palen.

Emperor Chengzong (reigned 1294-1307) recognized Zangpo Pal as the successor and ordered him to return to Tibet. Zangpo Pal had seven wives and 12 sons. He died in 1322 and the family contradictions again erupted. In 1325, Imperial Preceptor Kunga Lodro Gyaltsen, a son of Zangpo Pal, divided his stepbrothers into four dynastic houses: the Shithok, Lhakhang, Ringchengang, and Duchod dynastic houses. Among them, he distributed the power and honorific posts bestowed by the Yuan court. The Shithok house got the post of Sakya Monastery abbot, the Lhakhang house got the post of Imperial Preceptor, the Ringchengang house also got the inheritance rights to the post of Sakya Monastery abbot, and the Duchod house got the Prince Palen title. Under the chief abbot of Sakya Monastery, each dynastic house had its own abbot, a post that passed from father to son. Economically, each dynastic house had its own subjects, manors and fortress. The Sakya sect still enjoyed the great support of the Yuan court, and each dynastic house had high official posts. The Sakya sect therefore still dominated the 13 myriarchies of Ü-Tsang as before. However, later on, when the Sakya faced a hostile challenge from the Pagtru myriarchy, its weakness due to internal divisions was exposed, which made the Sakya sect fall apart quickly.

When the Sakya sect began to decline owing to intense rivalries within the Khon family, the Pagtru myriarchy in the Yarlung valley in Lhoka (Shannan) was growing stronger day by day under the leadership of Changchub Gyaltsen (1302-64) of the Lang family. In his youth, Changchub Gyaltsen had been sent to Sakya to be an attendant of Zangpo Pal and to study Buddhism and the administration of civil affairs. This was a traditional way in which the other myriarchs kept in contact with the Sakya sect. In 1322, Changchub Gyaltsen became the Pagtru myriarch. Under his rule, the local economy developed and troops were well trained. When Pagtru got stronger, Changchub Gyaltsen became determined to take back the lost land that had been seized by the Yazang myriarchy and that had originally been granted to Pagtru by the Yuan court. Pagtru's ownership of the land was stipulated in edicts issued by Kublai Khan through the Political Council (Xuanzheng Yuan). Changchub Gyaltsen's way of thinking was in line with Yuan Dynasty law and the wishes of Pagtru's people and manorial lords. After repeated failures over more than a decade, he defeated the Yazang myriarchy and recaptured the lost land. There had always been land disputes between Yazang and Pagtru.

The Sakya sect did not want to see Pagtru become stronger so, pretending to mediate in the dispute, it tried to suppress Pagtru. The Sakya sect several times tried to use legislative measures to dismiss Changchub Gyaltsen as governor but failed because of his resistance. In 1346, the Sakya *ponchen* Gyalwa Zangpo, collaborating with the Tsalpa myriarch and the Yamdrok myriarch, who also did not want to see a strong Pagtru, led troops in an attack on the town of Nedong, the Pagtru capital. When Changchub Gyaltsen and the Yazang myriarch were before the *ponchen*, the *ponchen* arrested Changchub Gyaltsen and tried to force Pagtru to cede Nedong. But because Changchub Gyaltsen and his men had prepared themselves well for the battle, the Sakya *ponchen* failed to seize Nedong. At that time, there was internal conflict within the Sakya sect, and Gyalwa Zangpo was dismissed as the Sakya *ponchen*. Changchub Gyaltsen was released as a result and he returned to Nedong.

In August 1348, the Sakya *ponchen* Wangtson, with a united army of troops from the Tsalpa, Yamdrok and other myriarchies, once again attacked Pagtru. Because their commanders were repeatedly removed during battle and bad commands were given, the Sakya troops were defeated by the Pagtru troops. Pagtru occupied a large part of Yazang's land. The Tsalpa myriarchy was forced to sue for peace by ceding part of its land. In 1350, Changchub Gyaltsen sent an envoy to the capital of the Yuan Dynasty to report on the situation to the emperor. The Yuan emperor recognized the power and status that Changchub Gyaltsen had achieved through his efforts and bestowed on him two silver seals of authority.

In 1353, Pagtru again defeated the Sakya, Tsalpa and Drigung troops. Using the Sakya's internal conflicts, Changchub Gyaltsen collaborated with Gyalwa Zangpo to attack Sakya, occupying Sakya Monastery and a large part of Ü-Tsang. The Pagtru sect subdued the Sakya sect and seized ruling power in Tibet. In 1358, Changchub Gyaltsen captured the Sakya *ponchen*'s official seal from the Sakya sect and, by order of the Yuan emperor, arranged for Imperial Preceptor Sonam Lodro to go on a journey to the Yuan capital, Beijing. In 1360, Changchub Gyaltsen sent Sherab Tashi to the capital to request the emperor for an honorific title. The Yuan Emperor Shundi bestowed on Changchub Gyaltsen a tiger-handled seal of authority and an edict giving him an honorific title, put Gongkar and Rinpung and other places in Ü and Tsang under Changchub Gyaltsen's control, and made Changchub Gyaltsen's assistant Shakya Rinchen the myriarch of Chumik. A grand ceremony was held in Nedong, the capital of the Pagtru regime, to announce the imperial edict to the Mongolian chief military commander and officials of the Ü-Tsang Pacification Commission. Soon afterward, in accordance with the Pagtru sect's traditions, a ceremony was held in Dansa Thel Monastery to celebrate the use by Changchub Gyaltsen of the new seal (which was equivalent to the Sakya *ponchen*'s seal). The ceremony symbolized that the Sakya regime had been replaced by the Pagtru regime.

During the Yuan Dynasty, Tibetan society was relatively stable and its economy developed greatly because the nation was unified. Tibetan science and culture made many achievements. Tibet experienced one of its most prosperous periods in the development of science, technology and culture. The development of Buddhism in the Yuan Dynasty, including the translation and annotation of sutras as well as the writing of theses on Buddhism, had a great impact on calendrical calculation, medicine, astronomy, art, literature and history in Tibet. It also had a great impact on the science and culture of later generations.

The local Sakya regime also paid great attention to the development of culture. When Phagpa was going to and fro between Sakya and the Chinese capital city of Dadu (now Beijing), he collected various classical and Buddhist books. At that time, monks going to Tibet from India, Kashmir and Nepal always brought some Buddhist scriptures. Phagpa had the books copied, translated, edited, and stored in Sakya. Some important sutras were copied with ink made of gold or precious stones so that they would last for a long time. Many Buddhist sutras were kept in the northern and southern Sakya monasteries. The southern Sakya Monastery alone had more than 60,000 volumes of Buddhist scriptures. Quite a few of them were rare and precious scriptures written on palm leaves and renowned for their beautiful calligraphy.

Several Tibetan versions of the Tripitaka were compiled during the Yuan Dynasty, of which the most famous was the Nartang edition Tripitaka compiled by Buton Rinchen Drup, along with the catalogues of *Tengyur* and *Kangyur* compiled by Tsalpa Kunga Dorje. These editions greatly influenced the compilation and block printing of the Tripitaka by later generations. With the support of Phagpa and other Sakya leaders, the *Kavyadarsa* (*Mirror of Poetry*), a theoretical work on rhetoric by the Indian scholar Dandin, was translated into Tibetan by Shodo Dorje Gyaltsen and others between 1260 and 1286. This was historically significant for Tibetan literature. When Tibetan students had absorbed the *Kavyadarsa*, a new genre of Tibetan literature gradually came into being – the Mirror of Poetry genre.

Music and fine arts also developed remarkably. *On Music* by Sakya Pandita Kunga Gyaltsen was a great achievement in this sphere. Sakya Monastery and Shalu Monastery, known for their architecture, sculpture and paintings, were the most prominent representative architectural works.

The mural "Phagpa Interviewing Kublai", the wall picture of Guhyasamaja (a deity of the supreme yogic tantras) of esoteric Buddhism in Sakya Monastery's Great Hall, and the remains of a mural of Hevajra (the Happy Thunderbolt, a deity of the supreme yogic tantras) in the Lolang Lhakhang temple of the southern Sakya Monastery are all works from the Yuan Dynasty. These exquisite paintings have traces of the art of central Asia and of China's hinterland. The most renowned Sakya Monastery murals are those of mandala patterns. It was recorded that, at the time of the *ponchen* Aglen Tashi, there were 639 mandala wall paintings on the top floor of the Sakya Monastery's Great Hall. These paintings influenced those in Shalu, Nartang and Kumbum monasteries, as well as those at Palkhor Chode Monastery built during the Ming Dynasty.

Shalu Monastery was rebuilt three times on different scales during the Yuan Dynasty. Its layout was finally settled during the period of Kunga Dondrup and Buton Rinchen Drup. Shalu Monastery was a Tibetan Buddhist monastery whose structure was influenced by Yuan palace art and the architectural style of China's hinterland. It was a typical mixture of Han and Tibetan architectural styles.

The incorporation of Tibet into China by the Yuan Dynasty put an end to the divisions that Tibet had experienced for more than 300 years after the collapse of the Tubo Dynasty. It brought about a unified and stable political situation in Tibet and made it possible for the Tibetan people to rehabilitate and restore their production. Tibet's incorporation into China promoted economic and cultural exchanges between Tibet and China's hinterland. Architectural skills and the skills of shipbuilding, pottery, and block printing, as well as the related materials, were introduced into Tibet from the hinterland. At the same time, Tibetan Buddhism and its culture and art spread to the hinterland and greatly influenced culture and art there. The new Mongolian script devised by Phagpa was widely used in the Yuan emperor's edicts and

A mandala of Amitabha.

A Buddhist ritual.

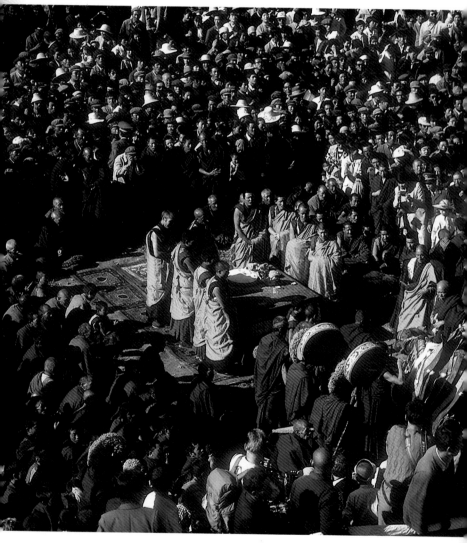

Frescoes on the walls in the Sakya Monastery assembly hall.

Sakya Monastery.

in official documents, seals, tablets, and coins. During the Yuan Dynasty, Beijing and Hangzhou became centers of Tibetan Buddhist artistic creation. Along with Tibetan Buddhism as such, Tibetan Buddhist art was introduced into the hinterland, including the art of building Buddhist pagodas and monasteries and stone and wooden sculpture. Some important cultural relics from this time still exist, such as the White Dagoba of Beijing's Miaoying Temple, the Cloud Terrace (Yuntai) at Juyongguan, and the stone sculptures of esoteric Buddhism on Hangzhou's Feilai Peak.

Tibet entered a new historical period when it was incorporated into China during the Yuan Dynasty. Monasteries from this period that are still extant include Sakya, Shalu, Tsurpu, Drigung, Taklung and Riwoqê monasteries. This period was characterized by the mutual influence of architecture between Tibet and the rest of China's hinterland, and the spread of Tibetan Buddhism and its culture into the hinterland. Many Tibetan cultural relics from this time still exist.

Sakya Monastery (Sakya County, Shigatse Prefecture)

Sakya Monastery comprises a northern and a southern monastery. The northern monastery is north of the river Drum Qu, on the southern slopes of

High walls and prayer wheels at Sakya Monastery.

Mount Benbo. The southern monastery is on a plain south of the Drum Qu.

The northern monastery was established in 1073 by Khon Konchok Gyalpo, founder of the Sakya sect. It was originally regarded as the main monastery of the Sakya sect. The monastery began to take on a political dimension in the 13th century when Sakya's fourth ruling lama, Sapan Kunga Gyaltsen, held power. After Kublai ascended the throne in 1260, he granted Phagpa the title of State Preceptor and ordered him to supervise the Buddhist affairs of the whole nation and preside over the administration of Tibet. In 1265, Phagpa returned to Sakya from the Yuan capital Dadu and began to prepare to set up a local regime in Tibet. The northern monastery became the location of Tibetan administrative organizations, so Phagpa had the monastery enlarged. The monastery was magnificent, with its buildings stretching along the hillside. Although it was destroyed, the northern monastery's ruins can still conjure up images of the splendor of its prime.

On Phagpa's orders, *Ponchen* Sakya Sangpo set up the southern monastery in 1268. It is square and covers an area of 50,000 square meters. The complex of monastic buildings is surrounded by a huge, thick square wall, with turrets on the four corners, a pathway on the top, and fortresses on the four sides. The wall is surrounded by a city moat.

The main buildings include Lhakhang Chenmo and Ngodrup Lhakhang. Lhakhang Chenmo, the assembly hall, is a square hall that can hold 10,000 monks. In the Ngodrup Lhakhang temple are 11 stupas of Sakya's ruling lamas, while the hall in its backyard houses a precious mural of the great political event that was the meeting between Sapan and Godan.

As Sakya Monastery was once the seat of the Tibetan local government, there are many historical relics, including edicts, seals, hats and clothes given by the central government to Sakya officials, as well as Buddhist images, religious instruments, and porcelain from the Song and Yuan dynasties. Many precious items are preserved in the monastery. To the rear of the assembly hall is a large library, while sutras cover all four walls of the hall. There are more than 10,000 sutras, generally copied by professional copyists gathered from throughout Tibet during Phagpa's rule. The sutras form a treasure-house of calligraphic skill in liquid gold and silver, cinnabar and black ink. The text of the *Kangyur* and *Tengyur* has been copied in ink made from golden powder and there are sutras written on palm leaves. There are also Tibetan books on astronomy, geography, calendrical calculations, medicine, literature, and history. Sakya Monastery has thus been praised as a "second Dunhuang."

Shalu Monastery (Shigatse County)

The distinctive green roof tiles of Shalu Monastery.

About 30 kilometers southeast of Shigatse in Tsongdu District is Shalu Monastery, a renowned Tibetan Buddhist monastery founded by Sherab Jungne in the early stages of Tibetan Buddhism's revival. Its architecture is distinctive, combining Han and Tibetan styles. The monastery consisted of a great hall, four *dratsangs* (colleges), and living quarters for monks. Now only the great hall still remains. It is a two-story building that faces east. The bottom floor consists of an assembly hall with an area of 1,500 square meters. There are images of Sakyamuni and his eight chief disciples inside. On two sides of the hall are chapels for housing the *Kangyur* and *Tengyur* sutras.

The upper floor consists of a main hall, a front hall, and two halls on the right and left that face each other. These are arranged like a Chinese-style courtyard. The green-tiled Chinese roof with upturned eaves and rafters is supported by carved brackets. Vivid designs of flying *apsara* goddesses, lions, tigers, and flowers on the glazed tiles and rafters highlight the simple Chinese architectural style of the halls. In the main hall are images of Sakyamuni and Buton Rinchen Drup, and various sizes of copper Kadam pagodas. The monastery's so-called precious treasures are

A gilded statue in Shalu Monastery.

A giant *tangka* of Buddha is ritually displayed.

preserved in the main hall and include a sutra block made of sandalwood, and a jar for keeping holy water. It is said that the water in the jar is always fresh, will not evaporate for decades, and will not change its flavor. The side halls are called "mandala halls," and their early Tibetan murals of mandalas are rich in content and unique in style. In the center of the front hall is an image of Sakyamuni flanked by 16 arhats. On the walls of the corridor are depictions of the seven treasures and eight auspicious symbols. Shalu's well-maintained murals represent Buddhist art from the Yuan Dynasty and had a great impact on mural painting in the late Yuan and early Ming dynasties.

Tsurpu Monastery (Doilungdêqên County, Lhasa Municipality)

About 60 kilometers west of Lhasa, in Tsurpu Gully in Gurong District, Doilungdêqên County, is Tsurpu Monastery, the main monastery of the Karma Kagyu sect, the Black Hat lineage of Tibetan Buddhism. The monastery was founded in 1189 by the first Karmapa, Dusum Khyenpa, and enlarged by Karma Pakshi, the second Karmapa. The enlarged Tsurpu – with its halls, images, pagodas, and the *Kangyur* copied in gold and silver ink – was more influential than Karma Dansa Monastery and thus became the seat of the Black Hat lineage, as it still is today. Its abbot was the ruling lama of the Golden-Brimmed Black Hat lineage. The monastery is also the cradle of the unique Tibetan Buddhist custom of lineages of incarnate lamas. The second Karmapa, Karma Pakshi, was the first incarnate lama of Tibetan Buddhism. The monastery was destroyed by an earthquake in 1410 and rebuilt in 1414. When the Gelugpa sect attained politico-religious power over Tibet and the Dalai Lama became the leader of all the Tibetan Buddhist sects, the local Tibetan government sent an official from the *yigtsang*, a government organ in charge of religious affairs, to the monastery to supervise its administration. In the 1980s, Tsurpu was repaired and its traditional Tsurpu Yashi festival was restored. Now the monastery is one of the cultural relics under the protection of the Tibet Autonomous Region.

Drigung Monastery (Maizhokunggar County, Lhasa)

Drigung Monastery, the main monastery of the Drigung Kagyu sect, is in the Shorong River valley, the Shorong being a tributary of the Lhasa River. A small monastery was first built on this site by Minyak Gomrin. Rinchen Pal rebuilt and enlarged it in 1179. The rebuilt Drigung Monastery grew in size until it had a main assembly hall surrounded by many white houses containing private rooms for meditation. On the mountain behind the monastery is a well-known site for sky burials, called Drigung Mandala. Tibetans consider it one of the two most renowned sky-burial sites in the world, the other site being in India. The monastery was destroyed in the 13th century due to strife between religious sects. It was gradually restored in the 17th century. A custom of Drigung Monastery and its branches, such as the Yangrigang and Detsong monasteries, was to perform the "thunderbolt dance" during traditional religious festivals. At Drigung Monastery, the dance was performed each year on the 28th and 29th days of the third month of the Tibetan calendar. Beginning in the second lunar month, the monks would chant sutras for a month, a colored mandala would be painted to be the palace of the tutelary deity, and a *lingga* would be prepared in the form of a human-like monster made of *tsampa* (roasted highland barley) to symbolize religious enemies. When the dance was performed on the 28th and 29th days of the third month, the *lingga* would be cut into pieces and destroyed in a fire, as a symbol that the religious enemies have been killed and that the Buddhist Dharma, like the rising sun, would protect all living beings. It is said that Drigung Monastery's thunderbolt dance originated in the religious struggle that took place in Tibet 700 years ago.

Taklung Monastery (Lhunzhub County, Lhasa)

Taklung Monastery is in Pondo, north of Lhasa. It was founded in 1180

Elderly Buddhist.

by the sage Taklung Thangpa Tashipal as a monastery of Tibetan Buddhism's Kagyu sect. In 1276, the monastery sent its monk Sangyewon to build a monastery in Riwoqê in Qamdo as a branch of Taklung Monastery. The Riwoqê monastery was called the "lower monastery," while its parent monastery, Taklung, became known as the "upper monastery." The Ming Emperor Chengzu granted the ninth abbot of Taklung Monastery, Tashi Paltseg, the title of State Preceptor, a silver seal of power and an imperial mandate. Some of the *tangka* paintings of the Yuan and Ming dynasties (1271-1644) that were originally kept in the two monasteries were taken to some US and European museums in the 20th century and they are highly esteemed by Western collectors, historians and artists. The *tangkas* are representative of the Tibetan art of that period.

Chapter 5

A Multitude of Monasteries Throughout Tibet

The Tibetan Policy of the Ming Court

When the Ming Dynasty was established in 1368, Tibet's secular and religious leaders gave allegiance to it. The Ming Emperor Taizu reorganized the administrative of Tibetan areas. In July 1374, the Ming court set up the Xi'an Regional Military Commission in Hezhou (today's Linxia County in Gansu), and promoted Wei Zheng, the Hezhou garrison commander, to the post of regional military commissioner to govern the Hezhou, Do-Kham and Ü-Tsang garrisons. The court later raised the status of the Do-Kham and Ü-Tsang garrisons to regional military commissions. In December 1374, State Preceptor Namgyel Palzang Pal and Sonam Odser, the associate administrator of the Xi'an Regional Military Commission, sent envoys to the Ming capital to pledge their allegiance and to recommend 56 local officials, including Changchub Gyaltsen, to the imperial court. Emperor Taizu thus set up the Do-Kham Pacification Commission, six bandit-suppression commissions, four *wanhu* or myriarchies (administrative units each covering 10,000 households), and 17 *qianhu* (comprising 1,000 households each). He appointed the Tibetan officials associate commanders, pacification commissioners, bandit-suppression commissioners, myriarchs and *qianhu* chieftains. The emperor sent the director Xu Yunde to grant each of the officials a seal of authority and a certificate of appointment.

The Ming Dynasty established the administrative system of a regional military commission with garrisons and battalions, and it appointed many local Tibetan officials to head these bodies. Documentary records of the Ming Dynasty and some Tibetan historical annals record many instances of Tibetan chieftains offering tribute and being given rewards. It can thus be seen that, at least during the first half of the Ming period, the administrative system of the regional military commission and garrisons and battalions was established in all Tibetan areas, including Ü-Tsang. At the time of Ming Emperor Yongle (reigned 1403-25), the Ming Dynasty, with its increased understanding of Tibetan areas, gave a great number of honorific titles to the local high-ranking monks who held power.

In areas inhabited by ethnic Han people, only the male members of the emperor's family could be granted the title of "prince" during the Ming Dynasty. Princes living outside the capital cities were called "regional princes." As a rule, they could not interfere in state and local administrative affairs. On the other hand, an official not from the royal family, even if he had accomplished a great deal, could be granted at most the title of marquis, but not that of prince. The local leaders of ethnic minorities who pledged allegiance to the Ming court could be granted the title of prince. For instance, some local leaders in Mongolia who held politico-military power were granted the title of prince by Ming emperors. However, Tibetan leaders with the Ming title of prince were different from the Mongolian leaders because they were not only local leaders but also Buddhist monks. They usually passed their title and power on to their sons, nephews or disciples. Therefore, their status was between that of a secular prince and that of the Prince of Dharma, a title granted by Ming emperors to a Tibetan Buddhist leader. They held local administrative and religious power, so the title conferred by the Ming court was related to Buddhism.

The Ming court also made use of the great influence of Buddhism on Tibet. It used the monastic system to enhance, through religion, the Ming's influence on Tibetan areas. The highest title conferred on Tibetan lamas by the Ming court was Prince of Dharma. Great Treasure Prince of Dharma was the title conferred by Emperor Yongle (also known as Emperor Chengzu) on Deshin Shekpa, the fifth Karmapa of the Karma Kagyu sect's Black Hat lineage.

A seal and inscription issued to a ruling lama by the Ming emperor.

The title Great Vehicle Prince of Dharma was conferred on the Sakya sect's leader. The title Son of Buddha of the Western Heaven was conferred on Shakya Yeshe, a high-ranking monk of the Gelugpa sect who was also granted the title of Great Mercy Prince of Dharma during the Xuande reign period (1426-35). Other titles included Great State Preceptor, State Preceptor and Chan Master.

In 1374, Namgyel Palzang Pal, the acting Imperial Preceptor of the former Yuan Dynasty, recommended 60 former Yuan officials, including Karmapa Rolpai Dorje, to the Ming Emperor Taizu. The emperor conferred on Rolpai Dorje the title of State Preceptor of Consecration. Rolpai Dorje, the fourth Karmapa, died in 1383. The fifth Karmapa was Deshin Shekpa (1384-1415), whose original name was Chopel

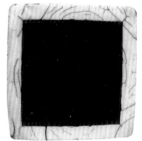

A seal and inscription issued to a State Preceptor by the Ming emperor.

Zangpo. Deshin Shekpa was a native of Nyangpo in Ü. At the age of four, he began to study Buddhism under the tutelage of Khakyod Wangpo, the second *tulku* or incarnate lama of the Karma Kagyu sect's Red Hat lineage. Deshin Shekpa was recognized as the reincarnation of Rolpai Dorje. When he was 18, Deshin Shekpa was held in high esteem and supported by Odser Namkha, a local leader of the Gonjo district of Kham. He preached in the Kham area and enjoyed a good reputation. The Ming Emperor Yongle, when he ascended the throne in 1403, sent the eunuch Hou Xian to invite Karmapa Deshin Shekpa for an audience. Deshin Shekpa arrived in Nanjing in 1407, during the first month of the Tibetan lunar calendar. He stayed in Linggu Monastery, where he and the monks set up 12 altars to pray for 14 days for the expiation of the sins of the emperor's dead parents. He had another altar built in the imperial palace to bestow "boundless consecration" on the emperor. He also gave sermons and translated sutras.

His Buddhist activities for the emperor were not ordinary activities because Emperor Yongle had come to the throne through military force by seizing imperial power from his nephew, Emperor Jianwen, and he was facing resistance and denunciation from the former emperor's supporters. He urgently needed the Karmapa's help to enhance his prestige and demonstrate his filial piety before the common people. That was why Emperor Yongle relied on and showed great respect to the Karmapa in such an exceptional way. The emperor conferred on the Karmapa the title of Great Treasure Prince of Dharma, entrusted him to supervise the whole nation's Buddhist affairs, and granted him a seal of authority, an imperial mandate, gold, silver, money, colored cotton and silk, a precious *kasaya* (a monk's outer vestment) decorated with pearls and jewels, gold and silver Buddhist implements, and a saddled horse.

After staying in Nanjing and on Mount Wutai for more than a year, Karmapa Deshin Shekpa bade farewell to the emperor. The emperor gave him gold and silver, colored cotton and silk, and images of Buddha, and had officials escort Deshin Shekpa back to Tibet. After returning to Tibet, the Karmapa offered the precious *kasaya* to the Jowo Buddha image and gave alms to all the Tibetan Buddhist monasteries in Ü-Tsang. Newupa, a manorial lord in Lhasa, offered him a monastery on the Potala Hill as his seat.

The Karmapa died on the 15th day of the eighth month in the wood-sheep year of the Tibetan lunar calendar (1415). The sixth incarnate lama of the Black Hat lineage, Tongwa Donden (1416-53), inherited the title of Great Treasure Prince of Dharma. He sent envoys to offer tribute to the Ming emperor eight times in the period between 1426 and 1450. The Ming court invited him to the capital but he failed to visit.

A *tangka* of a Dharma raja, given by the Ming emperor.

The Ming Emperor Yongle conferred the title of Great Vehicle Prince of Dharma on Kunga Tashi, the ruling lama of the Sakya sect's Duchod dynastic house. Kunga Tashi's grandfather was Kunga Gyaltsen Palzangpo, the Imperial Preceptor appointed by the Yuan Dynasty. Kunga Tashi's father was Dawen Lodro Gyaltsen. After Dawen Lodro Gyaltsen was defeated by his opponent Changchub Gyaltsen, the Sakya regime was forced to move to Datsang Dzong. Dawen Lodro Gyaltsen went to the Yuan capital of Dadu in 1356. The Yuan Emperor Shundi conferred on him the title of Great Yuan State

Preceptor of Prosperous Buddhism and appointed him tutor of the crown prince. Dawen Lodro Gyaltsen and Imperial Preceptor Lachen Sonam Lodro continued to bring accusations against the Da Situ, Changchub Gyaltsen, but without success. Dawen Lodro Gyaltsen died in 1359 in the city of Dadu.

Kunga Tashi began to study Buddhism as a child. He entered the monastic discipline in 1372 and studied Buddhist scriptures under the tutelage of Lama Tenpa Sonam Gyaltsen. He preached and went on pilgrimages to sacred places in various parts of Ü and Tsang, and became a representative of the Sakya family. His far-reaching reputation attracted the attention of the Ming Emperor Yongle, who twice sent envoys to invite him to the capital. At that time, Kunga Tashi was already an old man over the age of 60. However, despite other people's attempts to dissuade him, he decided to go to the capital. He left Sakya Monastery for the capital in 1412, the 10th year of the Yongle reign period. After a journey of 10 months, he arrived in Nanjing in the second month of the 11th year of the Yongle reign period (1413). He had an audience with the emperor, and preached many times. Emperor Yongle conferred on him the title of Great Vehicle Prince of Dharma of All Disciplines, Complete Combination, the Wonderful Law, Supreme Bhutatathata (Suchness), Great Mercy, Widespread Charity, the Preaching of Buddhism for the Country's Protection and Perfect Enlightenment, and the Buddha of Great Pervading Light and Virtuous Vajra of the Western Heaven (or Great Vehicle Prince of Dharma, for short). The emperor bestowed on him a gold seal of authority and an imperial mandate, by which the emperor put all of the nation's monks and its Buddhist affairs under his control. After visiting Beijing and Mount Wutai, Kunga Tashi returned to Nanjing, where he blessed and chanted sutras for the emperor. The emperor gave him silver statues of Hevajra and Yamantaka, Buddhist implements such as bells and *vajra* implements, Tripitaka sutras, monk's hats, *kasayas* (outer garments), gold and silver articles, silk, tents, tea, cattle, horses and mules. Kunga Tashi left the capital in 1414, during the first month of the year of the horse and returned to Sakya Monastery in the 12th month of the same lunar year. Another good outcome of his journey was that he persuaded the Ming Emperor Yongle to order the Pagtru regime to return Sakya Monastery to the Sakya sect. This was something that the Sakya sect had been trying to achieve for decades. In May 1413, the emperor sent a party headed by Hou Xian to Tibet to give the local leaders of Ü-Tsang imperial orders as well as a mandate in which the emperor ordered Pagtru Desi to return Sakya

The seal and inscription issued to the Karmapa by the Ming emperor.

Monastery to the Sakya sect. Hou Xian and his party arrived in Tibet in December. The Sakya sect held a grand ceremony for Hou Xian to declare the mandate. This event reflected the fact that the Ming Dynasty central government had decisive power when it came to solving disputes between Tibetan religious sects.

Shakya Yeshe, a representative of the Tibetan Buddhist Gelugpa sect, was granted the title of Great Mercy Prince of Dharma by the Ming Dynasty. On behalf of his tutor Tsongkhapa, the founder of the Gelugpa sect, Shakya Yeshe went to the capital and had an audience with the emperor. Before the Gelugpa sect was founded, Pagtru Desi, the Newu Dzongpon, and Ming envoys had reported to the Ming emperor on Tsongkhapa's Buddhist activities. Emperor Yongle sent out Hou Xian in 1403 to invite Karmapa Deshin Shekpa to an audience and he conferred on Pagtru Desi Drakpa Gyaltsen the title of Propagation Prince of Persuasion in 1406. At about the same time, the emperor sent out envoys to hand an invitation letter to Tsongkhapa. In the sixth month of the earth-rat year in the seventh cycle of the Tibetan calendar (1408), Tsongkhapa wrote a letter of reply, saying that he sincerely thanked the emperor for his invitation and many gifts but unfortunately could not go to the capital. In the second month of the 11th year of the Yongle reign period (1413), the emperor again sent Hou Xian to invite Tsongkhapa to an audience. Tsongkhapa explained in detail to the envoy why he could not go to the capital and asked the envoy to take back to the emperor his letter of reply and many gifts. In these circumstances, it is possible that the imperial envoy asked Tsongkhapa to send one of his disciples to the emperor as a representative, so Shakya Yeshe went to the capital as a representative of Tsongkhapa.

When Shakya Yeshe arrived in the suburbs of Beijing in November 1413, he was warmly welcomed by officials led by the capital city's military commander and escorted to where he would stay – Haiyin Monastery by Lianhua (Lotus) Pond. Shakya Yeshe had an audience with the emperor at the imperial palace's Dashan (Great Virtue) Hall. The emperor was pleased to see him, held a welcome banquet for him, and gave him gifts on several occasions. In April 1415, the emperor conferred on Shakya Yeshe the title Buddha's Son of Western Heaven, Great State Preceptor of Wonderful Enlightenment, Complete Combination of Wisdom and Mercy, and Widespread Buddhist Consecration and Mercy. According to Tibetan annals, Shakya Yeshe cured the emperor's illness using Tibetan medicine and Tibetan Buddhist rituals. He also had six monasteries built on Mount Wutai. The monks in these six monasteries practiced the Gelugpa sect's form of Tibetan Buddhism.

In 1416, Shakya Yeshe returned to Tibet with the first cinnabar block-printed edition of the Tripitaka's *Kangyur* printed in a Han area, along with a painting of himself with words of praise written by the emperor. These are now precious cultural relics. This edition of the *Kangyur* had a great influence on the development of block printing and on Tibetan culture in Tibetan areas. It is kept now in Sera Monastery. After he returned to Tibet, Shakya Yeshe offered Master Tsongkhapa a large amount of treasure that he had brought from the Han area. In 1419, Tsongkhapa went to Sera Choding and asked Shakya Yeshe to build a big monastery there. Sera Monastery began to be built that year, with Shakya Yeshe in charge. Newu Dz-

Religious instruments given to Tibet's local government by the Ming central government: a *vajraghanta* ("diamond bell") and a *vajra* ("thunderbolt").

ongpon Namkha Sangpo provided a large part of the building costs. The treasure that Shakya Yeshe had brought back from the Han area also played an important role.

Shakya Yeshe again went to Beijing in May 1425. There, he took the lead in giving donations for the construction of Fahai Temple (Sea of Dharma Temple). To this day, a tablet still stands in Fahai Monastery with his name listed first among the donors. After living in Beijing for 10 years, he died in 1435 at the age of 82 on his way back to Tibet.

During the period between Emperor Yongle's reign (1403-25) and Emperor Xianzong's reign (1465-87), the Ming emperors granted Tibetan Buddhist leaders various honorific titles, such as Great Treasure Prince of Dharma, Great Vehicle Prince of Dharma, Great State Preceptor, and State Preceptor. All of these titles were not only honorific titles but also indications of official rank. Generally, a Great State Preceptor is at the fourth-highest rank, a State Preceptor is at the fifth rank, and a Chan Master at the sixth rank. The titleholders also received salaries. Numerous Tibetan Buddhist monks who came to Beijing and stayed there were given salaries by the Court of Imperial Entertainment. The Ming Emperor Yingzong (reigned 1435-49) also granted honorific titles to Tibetan Buddhist monks. The number of titles reached its peak during the Ming Emperor Xianzong's reign (1465-87), Emperor Xiaozong's reign period (1488-1505), and Emperor Wuzong's reign (1506-21). In 1487, the last year of Xianzong's Chenghua reign period, dozens of posts and titles were granted to Tibetan monks at the same time. Emperor Wuzong built a house called Bao Fang (Leopard House), where he and Tibetan monks chanted and studied sutras together, so that some records say that the emperor could speak the Tibetan language. He even granted himself a gold seal and the title of Great Celebrated Dharma Lord, the Ishvara Buddha of Wisdom and Complete Enlightenment in the Western Heaven. He sent the eunuch Liu Yun to Tibet in the 10th year of the Zhengde reign period (1515) to give gifts to high-ranking monks and to invite *tulkus* (incarnate lamas) to the capital. Liu Yun's journey to Tibet exhausted his manpower and financial resources and caused a great deal of trouble to the places through which he passed but his mission resulted in nothing but failure. During the Ming Emperor Shizong's Jiaqing reign period (1522-66), there was a decline in the activities of Tibetan Buddhist monks in Beijing because the emperor was a Taoist and discriminated against Tibetan Buddhism.

When the Pagtru regime held dominant power over Tibet during the Ming Dynasty, the Sakya sect still controlled some places in Tsang, such as Gyirong and Lhazê. Da Situ Changchub Gyaltsen stipulated many rules for the Pagtru regime. For example, the office of Pagtru Desi should be held by a monk from the Lang family who had been the abbot of Tsethang Monastery, while the office of Dzongpon should be held in rotation by a meritorious official to guarantee the regime's centralized power. The third Desi Chen-nga, Drakpa Changchub, who was born in 1356 and became the *chen-nga* (abbot) of Dansa Thel Monastery in 1371, was originally not qualified to be the Desi. However, the Pagtru council asked him to assume the post concurrently with that of abbot after the second Desi, Shakya Gyaltsen, died in 1373, so Drakpa Changchub promised to be the Desi concurrently until his stepbrother Sonam Drakpa came of age. Drakpa Changchub was therefore called Lapon (meaning someone who concurrently held the posts of Pagtru Desi and *chen-nga* or abbot of Dansa Thel Monastery). In 1381, he helped Sonam Drakpa become Pagtru Desi, while he himself remained the Dansa Thel abbot.

Due to internal struggles within the ruling Pagtru clique, the fourth Desi, Sonam Drakpa, resigned his position as Desi and resumed the post of Dansa Thel abbot. However, he resigned as abbot in 1405, withdrew from the world and became a hermit.

The fifth Pagtru Desi, Drakpa Gyaltsen, had the honorific title Propagation Prince of Persuasion. He changed some systems and rules, especially the family hereditary system for the office of Dzongpon, so that some families became aristocratic families with feudal manors, such as the Rinpungpa, Chongyepa, Newupa and Drakarwa families. To maintain control by strengthening the feudal ruling clique's hierarchy, Drakpa Gyaltsen stipulated that officials wear different clothing and ornamentation in accordance with their different ranks and that meetings between officials be conducted according to certain rites.

After Drakpa Gyaltsen died in 1432, strife erupted in the Lang family of the Pagtru ruling clique. Sangye Gyaltsen, the father of the sixth Desi, Drakpa Jungne, tried to seize his son's position. This sparked riots in 1434. Some aristocratic families took the opportunity to seize political power. After taking up his new post of Desi, Drakpa Jungne left the monastic life, returned to the secular world and got married. Thus, the rule formulated by Changchub Gyaltsen that the post of Pagtru Desi should be filled by a monk was violated. Since then, all those who have been Pagtru Desi have been laymen. The post of Pagtru Desi became hereditary. The Rinpungpa family, the strongest of the aristocratic families, with its seat in Rinpung in the Tsang region, controlled the Pagtru regime through matrimonial ties with the Pagtru family. The Rinpungpa family caused several civil wars. The Pagtru family was later divided into a Nedong branch and a Gongkar branch so, during the middle and end of the Ming Dynasty, Tibet experienced endless conflict and war between various local authorities. This situation lasted until the Desi Tsangpa rose up in Shigatse and established the Desi Tsangpa regime, which lasted for a brief period.

Another great event in Tibetan history during the Ming Dynasty was the founding and development of the Gelugpa or Yellow Hat sect. Tsongkhapa, the sect's founder, was from Tsongkha (the present-day Huangzhong County in Qinghai Province). He became a monk at the age of seven and went to Lhasa to study Buddhism when he was 16. He studied under the dozens of eminent monks of various sects. Having achieved a good command of Buddhist doctrine, he took disciples and propagated his views on Buddhism. Supported by the Propagation Prince of Persuasion, with the support of l.c Drakpa Gyaltsen of the Pagtru regime, and the Newu Dzongpon, Namkha Sangpo, he founded the Mönlam festival of prayer in the first month of the Tibetan New Year in 1409. Later that year, he founded Ganden Monastery, from which came the Gelugpa sect. The sect declared that it was a successor to the Kadampa sect founded by Atisha and Drom Tonpa. Many monasteries of the Kadampa sect converted to the Gelugpa sect, so the Gelugpa sect grew very quickly. Before Tsongkhapa died, his disciple Tashi Palden founded Drepung Monastery in 1416 and Shakya Yeshe, another disciple, founded Sera Monastery in 1419. Those two monasteries and

Sera Monastery monks debating.

Ganden Monastery were known as the three great monasteries of Lhasa. They were the basis of the Gelugpa sect in its early stages. Tsongkhapa died in 1419, at which time the sect did not have a system of reincarnation in place to determine the succession of its leader. Tsongkhapa was succeeded in his position as ruling lama, known as Ganden Tripa, by

his disciples Gyaltsab Je (the second Ganden Tripa) and Khedrup Je (the third Ganden Tripa and first Panchen Lama). Not long afterward, the newly emerging Gelugpa sect reached a low point when it was attacked by the Rinpungpa family.

At that time, Gedun Druppa (1391-1474, retrospectively named the first Dalai Lama), a disciple of Tsongkhapa, founded Tashilhunpo Monastery in Shigatse. The monastery became Gelugpa sect's base in Tsang. When Gedun Druppa died, he was succeeded as Tashilhunpo abbot by a disciple. But some people thought that Gendun Gyatso (1475-1542, the second Dalai Lama) was the reincarnation of Gedun Druppa and invited Gendun Gyatso to live in Tashilhunpo Monastery. As the Gelugpa sect had no reincarnation system, Gendun Gyatso's incarnation status could not be established. As the abbot of Tashilhunpo, Yeshe Tsemo, discriminated against him, Gendun Gyatso left Tashilhunpo for Drepung Monastery. He preached in Ü and enjoyed a good reputation. He founded Chokhorgyal Monastery in Shannan. In 1512, Yeshe Tsemo asked him to return to Tashilhunpo to be its abbot. This demonstrated that, in the Gelugpa sect, the reincarnation system had gained the upper hand over the master-disciple succession. Rinpungpa then prohibited the Gelugpa sect's monks from taking part in the Mönlam festival held in Lhasa during the first month. However, the Rinpungpa forces were driven out of Lhasa by the Pagtru forces not long afterward. The monks of Drepung Monastery asked Gendun Gyatso to return from Tashilhunpo. In 1517, Gendun Gyatso became the Drepung abbot. In 1518, he presided over the Mönlam festival and won back the Gelugpa monks' right to take part in it. In 1525, he concurrently took on the post of Sera Monastery abbot. In later generations, each of his successors would concurrently be abbot of both Drepung and Sera monasteries. He enjoyed greater prestige than the Ganden Tripa and became the actual leader of the Gelugpa sect. The Newu Dzongpon granted him a manor, which was renamed Ganden Potrang (Ganden Palace).

Sonam Gyatso (1543-88), the third Dalai Lama and the incarnation of Gendun Gyatso, promoted the further development of the Gelugpa sect. When Mongolian armed forces entered the Qinghai-Tibet Plateau, Sonam Gyatso went from Lhasa to Qinghai at the invitation of Altan Khan, the chieftain of the Mongol Tumet tribe. They met by Lake Qinghai. Altan Khan conferred on Sonam Gyatso the honorific title of All-Knowing Vajra-Holder Dalai Lama. This was the origin of the title Dalai Lama (Ocean Lama). Later, the hierarchy of the Gelugpa sect posthumously conferred the title of first Dalai Lama on Gedun Druppa and the title of second Dalai Lama on Gendun Gyatso. The title of third Dalai Lama went to Sonam Gyatso. When the Ming rulers found out that the Mongol khan held Sonam Gyatso in great respect, they asked Sonam Gyatso to persuade Altan Khan to with-

The inscription for the title of Dorje Chang that was granted to the third Dalai Lama by the Ming government in 1588.

draw his men back to Mongolia. The khan heeded his advice, so the Ming conferred on Sonam Gyatso the title of Dorje Chang (Vajra Holder) when he went to Hohhot in 1586 to preside over Altan Khan's funeral ceremony and invited him to Beijing. The Dalai Lama accepted the invitation and left for the Ming capital but death intervened and he died in 1588 on his way to Beijing.

Altan Khan's great-grandson Yonten Gyatso (1589-1616) was identified by the Gelugpa sect and the Mongol Tumet tribe as the incarnation of Sonam Gyatso. Escorted by a Mongol armed unit and aristocrats, Yonten Gyatso went to Tibet and was enthroned as the fourth Dalai Lama. He was the only Dalai Lama of Mongol origin. His Mongol background was of great support to the Gelugpa sect, which was then being suppressed by the newly emerging Desi Tsangpa. Yonten Gyatso was ordained by his sutra tutor, Lozang Choskyi Gyaltsen (1570-1662), the abbot of Tashilhunpo Monastery. The status of Lozang Choskyi Gyaltsen thus increased greatly in Tashilhunpo Monastery and the Gelugpa sect. Since then, the position of Tashilhunpo abbot has been held by Lozang Choskyi Gyaltsen and his successors, from whom came the Panchen Lama lineage, another important *tulku* incarnation lineage of the Gelugpa sect.

The fourth Dalai Lama died in 1616. The Desi Tsangpa, taking advantage of his victory in a battle against the Lhasa chieftain Kyishodpa, a supporter of the Gelugpa sect, banned any search for the Dalai Lama's reincarnation and confiscated the land and subjects of Drepung and Sera monasteries. The Gelugpa sect appealed to the Mongol Tumet tribe for help. Tumet troops defeated the Desi Tsangpa. When Desi Tsangpa Phuntsok Namgyel died, his successor Desi Tsangpa Karma Tenkyong Wangpo was only 16 years old. The subordinates of the new Desi held different opinions on the problem of searching for the Dalai Lama's reincarnation. It was only after repeated pleas by Lozang Choskyi Gyaltsen that Karma Tenkyong Wangpo lifted the ban and the search began. The fifth Dalai Lama was thus identified and was enthroned at Drepung Monastery.

Tibetan opera.

In 1630, Linden Khan of the Mongol Chahar tribe, which was suppressed by the Jin Dynasty, moved west, defeated the Tumet tribe, and moved to Qinghai. In this dangerous situation, the head of the Gelugpa sect, Depa Sonam Rabten, appealed for help to the leader of the Hoshot Mongols, whose army was stationed in Xinjiang. The Hoshot leader Gushri Khan was then a follower of the Gelugpa sect. In 1636, Gushri Khan led his forces in an attack on Qinghai. He occupied Qinghai and Kham between 1637 and 1639. In 1642, he took the war into Tibet, seized Shigatse and put an end to the Desi Tsangpa regime. He established the Ganden Potrang regime, which was ruled jointly by the Hoshot tribe and Gelugpa sect.

In summary, in carrying out a policy of granting honorific titles to the leaders of all Tibetan Buddhist sects, the Ming Dynasty showed the sects respect, conferring on the leaders and their disciples titles such as Great Treasure Prince of Dharma, Great Vehicle Prince of Dharma, Great State Preceptor, and State Preceptor. Therefore, Ming rule over Tibet helped all the Tibetan Buddhist sects prosper. The emergence and development of the Gelugpa sect in particular had a great influence on Tibetan history. The cultural highlights of this period were the numerous new monasteries, of which those of the Gelugpa sect are representative. These can be found in many places in Tibet and include the three great monasteries of Lhasa (the Ganden, Sera, and Drepung), Tashilhunpo Monastery in Tsang, Champa Ling Monastery in Qamdo, Palkhor Chode Monastery in Shigatse, Samding Monastery in Tsang, and the Phagpa Lhakhang temple in Gyirong. The monasteries mentioned still exist and are worth visiting.

Ganden Monastery (Dagzê County, Lhasa)

Ganden Monastery's Tibetan name is Ganden Nampar Gyalwai Ling, which means "Monastery of the Pure Land of Tushita." In Chinese, it is also called Jile Si (Pure Land Monastery) or Jushan Si (Endowing Goodness Monastery). It is located at the foot of Mount Drokri in Tibet's Dagzê County. Founded by Tsongkhapa, Ganden is the chief monastery of the Gelugpa sect's six great monasteries. On the first day of the first month of the Tibetan calendar in the sixth year of the Yongle reign period (1409), Tsongkhapa

A fresco in Ganden Monastery.

first held the famous annual Mönlam prayer festival, which was attended by 800 monks. After the prayer festival, he decided to build his own monastery. He selected Mount Drokri as the site. Several buildings were completed in the space of a year, including a great hall and living quarters for the monks. Tsongkhapa held an inauguration ceremony for Ganden Monastery on February 5, 1410. He was the first Ganden Tripa (Throne Holder of Ganden). Ganden later expanded into a magnificent complex of buildings, but it never had more than 3,300 monks at any one time. The Ganden Tripa was next in

Ganden, the main monastery of the Gelugpa sect.

Ganden Monastery's newly repaired assembly hall.

Drepung Monastery's *tsogchen* (assembly hall).

status only to the Dalai Lama and Panchen Lama.

Ganden Monastery has about 50 buildings, including the *tsogchen* (assembly hall), Yangpachen Temple, the Sutra Hall, the Tri Dok Khang (Residence of the Throne Holder of Ganden), Ngam Cho Khang, Jangtse Dratsang (College), and Shartse Dratsang (College). The assembly hall, the largest hall in the monastery, was built in 1409, fitted with a gold roof in 1720, and expanded in 1749. The three-story building covers a total

Drepung Monastery.

area of 2,000 square meters, big enough for 3,000 monks to chant sutras inside. In the hall are images of Maitreya and Tsongkhapa, and Tsongkhapa's five-lion golden throne. Yangpachen Temple, built in 1416, comprises the Protector, Guru and Mandala prayer halls, Ser Dung Khang, and the Hall of Stupas of successive Tripas. Ser Dung Khang is the hall containing Tsongkhapa's stupa. Tsongkhapa's remains are entombed inside this silver stupa decorated with jewels. The 50th Tripa, Gendun Phuntsok, had the stupa plastered with gold, and the 13th Dalai Lama had it rebuilt. The splendid and magnificent rebuilt stupa was unfortunately destroyed in 1969. The stupa that can be seen now was built from the ruins in 1981.

Other prayer halls contain golden statues of Vijaya, Sitapata (the White Umbrella Goddess), and Manjushri. Tsongkhapa's chamber contains his sutra books, seals and other objects. There are many cultural relics of the Ming and Qing dynasties in the monastery, the most precious of which are a suit of armor and 24 embroidered silk *tangkas* given to Tsongkhapa by the Qing Emperor Qianlong in July 1757.

Drepung Monastery (Lhasa)

Drepung literally means "mound of rice," a name that well describes the first visual impression of the monastery. Painted mainly in white, Drepung Monastery lies on the slope of Mount Gephel-usel, west of the city of Lhasa. Its complete name is Pelden Drepung Chothan Jadla Nampar Gyalwai Ling. Jamyang Choje, a disciple of Tsongkhapa, founded the monastery in 1416 (the 14th year of the Yongle reign during the Ming Dynasty). At first, it consisted of only a handful of buildings that housed a few monks. Drepung soon grew into the largest of all the Gelugpa sect's monasteries, sometimes housing as many as 10,000 monks. With an area of 250,000 square meters, Drepung is the largest monastery in Tibet. With its buildings scattered on the hillside, it looks like a city from a distance. Its main buildings

Stone carvings on the circumambulation path around Drepung Monastery.

Drepung Monastery's assembly hall.

are the Great Assembly Hall, Ganden Potrang (Palace), four *dratsangs* (colleges), and 29 *khangtsens* (residential compounds for monks). The Great Assembly Hall is the monastery's largest building. The ground floor of the hall consists of a spacious room with 190 pillars and it can house nearly 10,000 monks. This is where the Drepung monks chant sutras and hold ceremonies. The floor above is dedicated to the Champa (Jowo) Buddha, whose statue is the monastery's main Buddha image. Tsongkhapa himself presided over the inauguration ceremony for the statue. In the Maitreya Prayer Hall on the third floor is a conch shell with clockwise spirals that Tsongkhapa gave to Jamyang Choje, Drepung's founder. In the room to the side are two silver stupas containing the relics of the third and fourth Dalai Lamas respectively. The biggest of Drepung's colleges is Loseling, which can house 4,000 or 5,000 monks. Each college has its own assembly hall, which is where collective chanting takes place. The statue of Yamantaka enshrined in the Ngagpa Dratsang (College of Esoteric Tibetan Buddhism) contains the remains of the translator Ra Lotsawa, one of the most important figures in the Yamantaka tradition. Ganden Potrang was the home and office of the third, fourth and fifth Dalai Lamas. This shows that Drepung was the most important of the Gelugpa sect's monasteries. Other Drepung prayer halls are dedicated to Tsongkhapa and his disciples, as well as to Avalokiteshvara, Manjushri, Vajra, Amitayus, Tara, and so on. Drepung has a great many Buddhist sutras, religious instruments, ceremonial articles, *tangka* paintings, murals and various handicraft items. Drepung has had a great influence on Tibetan Buddhist monasteries.

Sera Monastery (Lhasa)

The name Sera literally means "wild rose." The monastery got this name because wild roses grew on the site. Sera Monastery is in the north of Lhasa, along the base of Mount Sera-usel. It was founded by

Sera Monastery.

Sera Monastery.

The assembly hall of a Sera Monastery *dratsang* (college).

Tsongkhapa's disciple Shakya Yeshe in 1418, the 16th year of the Ming Dynasty's Yongle reign period. Shakya Yeshe was originally one of Tsongkhapa's personal attendants and he studied Buddhist scriptures very hard under Tsongkhapa's tutelage. He went to the capital in Tsongkhapa's stead in 1418. The emperor granted him an audience and the title of Great State Preceptor. After returning, he founded Sera Monastery in the same year by order of Tsongkhapa. He went to the capital again in 1434, the ninth year of the Xuande reign period. The Ming Emperor Xuanzong granted him the title Great Compassion Prince of Dharma. Sera consists of the assembly hall (*tsogchen*), three colleges (Me Dratsang, Ngagpa Dratsang and Je Dratsang), and 29 *khangtsen* (residential compounds). The magnificent assembly hall is the monastery's largest hall and has an area of 1,000 square meters. The number of monks was limited to 5,500 in the 17th century but it grew to 9,000 in the 1950s. The Buddha images in Sera are tall. The statue of Maitreya in the main hall and those of the eight great

Sera Monastery.

bodhisattvas in the back room are exquisite. The monastery has many cultural relics, its rare treasures including the 108-volume Tripitaka and set of 16 arhat statues given to Shakya Yeshe by Emperor Yongle, and a silk portrait of Shakya Yeshe made by order of Emperor Xuanzong. There are also 10,000 gilded copper Buddha statues, sutras, religious implements, murals and *tangka* paintings, all made in Tibet.

Palkhor Chode Monastery (Gyangzê County, Shigatse)

Palkhor Chode, a renowned Tibetan Buddhist monastery in Gyangzê, was founded between 1418 and 1436 by Rabten Kunzang and the first Panchen Lama, Khedrup Je. The monastery is now a cultural site protected by the Tibet Autonomous Region.

The monastery lies on a hillside. It consists of Gyangzê Kumbum, a three-story assembly hall (*tsogchen*), *dratsangs* (colleges), living quarters, and walls. The Gyangzê Kumbum and the assembly hall are its main

The chapels and pagoda of Palkhor Chode Monastery. The monastery has a collection of 1,049 sets of scriptures.

Tibetan scriptures in Palkhor Chode Monastery.

buildings. The assembly hall is a three-story building in the center of the monastery. Built in the Ming Dynasty, it faces south and has a cross-shaped plan. It is remarkably well preserved and many of the statues and paintings inside date back to when the monastery was founded. On the ground floor are the assembly hall itself, a winding corridor, the Protector Prayer Hall (east of the assembly hall) and the Vajradhatu Prayer Hall (west of the assembly hall). On the middle floor are a corridor, the Lamdre Prayer Hall (Prayer Hall of the Path and its Result), the Arhats Prayer Hall, and the Lhakyi Hall. On the top floor is the Zhelye Tse Prayer Hall (Prayer Hall of the Celestial Mansion Peak). All of these prayer halls were built between 1418 and 1425.

The Gyangzê Kumbum (popularly known as the Palkhor Chörten) is the monastery's most magnificent building. It covers an area of 2,200 square meters and was built between 1427 and 1436. It has 77 prayer halls and shrines and 100,000 statues and images, so it is also called "*chörten* (stupa) with 100,000 Buddha statues." It is a 13-story building consisting of four parts: a base, belly, neck and top. It has 108 doors and 72 rooms. Architecturally, it is a wonderful sight. The structure is not only imposing and splendid but also practical. It reflects the brilliant achievements of 15th-century Tibetan architecture.

In the Gyangzê Kumbum and the assembly hall are numerous splendid murals and beautiful statues. Motifs of esoteric Buddhism can be found in the assembly hall's Vajradhatu and Zhelye Tse prayer halls. In corridors and other halls, the mural motifs tell stories about Buddha and eminent monks. Except for the east and west chapels on the bottom floor and the prayer hall on the 4th floor, all of the Gyangzê Kumbum's prayer halls reflect the mandalas of the four parts of esoteric Buddhism. The murals and statues are of a very high artistic level and represent Tibetan Buddhist art at its prime.

Tashilhunpo Monastery.

Tashilhunpo Monastery (Shigatse)

One of the six great monasteries of the Gelugpa sect, Tashilhunpo Monastery is 2 or 3 kilometers west of the city of Shigatse, at the southern base of Mount Drolma. It is a key cultural site under state protection.

The monastery was founded in September 1447 by Gedun Druppa, the first Dalai Lama and one of Tsongkhapa's foremost disciples. The monastery was dedicated to Jowo Buddha, a statue of whom Gedun Druppa had made in memory of Sherab Senge, his sutra teacher. Gedun Druppa was the monastery's first abbot until his death in 1474.

Gedun Druppa was succeeded as abbot by one disciple after another. In 1601, the fourth Panchen Lama, Lozang Choskyi Gyaltsen, became abbot. The post was thereafter held only by successive Panchen Lamas, so that the monastery became the Panchen Lama's seat. New extensions to the monastery were built during the time of the fourth, fifth and sixth Panchen Lamas until Tashilhunpo grew into the vast monastery it is today. The monastery includes an assembly hall (*tsogchen*), a *lhakhang* (temple), the Jowo Prayer Hall, and the Sunning of the Buddha Platform. In the north and south are *dratsangs* (colleges) and *mitsen* (dormitory facilities).

In the south of the monastery are fruit orchards. The east of the orchards was originally the site of the former Panchen Lama's council of *khenpos* (learned abbots). The assembly hall is the monastery's oldest building. Nine rooms wide and seven rooms long, the hall contains 48 pillars. It is the main location for sermons and other activities involving the whole monastery. There is a throne for the Panchen Lama in the hall. In the north of the hall is the Sakyamuni

Prayer Hall, which is flanked by the Maitreya and Tara prayer halls. The Protector Prayer Hall is in the west of the hall. To the east of the assembly hall is a spacious courtyard of 600 square meters, where sutras are debated and where the Panchen Lama gives sermons to monks. Outside the assembly hall are four *dratsangs*: Tosangling, Shartse, Jikang and Ngapa. Each *dratsang* consists of prayer halls, shrines, a kitchen, a debating chamber, and living quarters for the *tulkus* (incarnate lamas).

The Jowo Buddha (Sakyamuni) Prayer Hall is in the western part of the monastery. It was founded in 1904 by the ninth Panchen Lama. Its very expensive construction used more than 8,000 ounces of gold. The prayer hall is 30 meters high, and its rectangular base covers 800 square meters, with a small courtyard inside. It houses a gilded statue of a sitting Jowo Buddha, consisting of five parts – the lotus throne, waist, chest, face and crown. The five parts are five stories connected by wooden staircases. The statue is 26.4 meters tall overall, with the body being 22.4 meters tall and the throne 3.8 meters tall. It is one of the tallest Buddha statues in China.

The Sunning of the Buddha Platform in the monastery's northeastern corner is very large, being 35 meters tall from the base and more than 40 meters wide. It was built with stone in 1468 to commemorate Sakyamuni's birth, enlightenment and nirvana. Each year, on the 15th day of the fourth month of the Tibetan lunar calendar, a giant *tangka* is ceremoniously displayed on the platform for worshipers to pay homage to Buddha.

There are prayer halls dedicated to the stupas of the fourth to ninth Panchen Lamas. The oldest was the Chokangsha Prayer Hall, which housed the stupa of the fourth Panchen Lama, Lozang Choskyi Gyaltsen. The stupa is 11 meters high and similar in form to that of the Dalai Lama. Coated with silver and decorated with jewels, it looks lively and splendid. The prayer hall's roof gleams with golden tiles arranged in a Chinese style. Construction began in 1662, the sixth year of the Qing Emperor Kangxi's reign, and finished four years later.

The stupa of the fourth Panchen Lama is now kept in the prayer hall housing the fifth Panchen Lama's stupa.

The Stupa Hall in Tashilhunpo Monastery.

West of the stupa halls is the Han Buddhist Prayer Hall Gyana Lhakhang, which was built during the Qing Emperor Qianlong's reign by the seventh Panchen Lama, Tenpai Nyima. This prayer hall houses a picture of Emperor Qianlong, in front of which is a tablet with the words, "A long, long life to Emperor Daoguang." This demonstrates Tsang's subordination to the Qing Dynasty's central government. The next room is an audience hall, where Qing ministers announced imperial edicts to the Panchen Lama. In the hall now, there is an exhibition of gifts given to the Panchen Lama by emperors, which include gold-leaf albums and gold seals, jade-leaf albums and jade seals, Buddha statues from the Sui and Tang dynasties, porcelain from the Ming Emperor Yongle's reign, sutras written on palm leaves, and brocade from the Yuan and Ming dynasties.

Champa Ling Monastery (Qamdo)

Champa Ling, also known as Qamdo Monastery, is the Gelugpa sect's largest and most renowned monastery. It is in Qamdo, an important town in eastern Tibet, and located on an island between the Za Qu and Ngom Qu rivers. According to the Gelugpa sect's rules, Champa Ling was entitled to house 2,500 monks.

Champa Ling has many subsidiary monasteries, of which about 100 are in the Kham region. Most of them are concentrated in Qamdo, Chagyab, Baxoi, Shopamdo, Sangngacho and Bomê.

The monastery has many murals, statues, sutras and other artistic treasures. The monastery's monks engage not only in religious activities but also in trade. With the profits, they buy everyday items such as butter, *tsampa* (barley flour), and tea, and distribute these items among all the monks. In 2003, the 11th Phagpalha Hutuktu (incarnation of the Living Buddha), Gelek Namgyel, became vice-chairman of the 10th National Committee of the Chinese People's Political Consultative Conference.

Samding Monastery (Nanggarzê County, Shannan)

Samding, a monastery of the Shangpa Kagyu sect, is on a cliff southwest of Lake Yamdrok in Nanggarzê County. It is more than 300 years old. It was probably founded by Khetsun Zhonu Drup, the fourth-generation disciple of Khyungpo Naljorpa, the founder of the Shangpa Kagyu sect, but other sources say the monastery was founded by the eminent lama Bodong Chokle Namgyel (1375-1451) in the early 15th century. The monastery was headed by an abbess but monks made up the rest of the community. It was most noted for its being headed by Dorje Pagmo, Tibet's only female incarnate lama. Her incarnation lineage has been passed down to the 12th generation.

In the 18th century, the monastery had an abbess and 80 monks. The number of monks increased to 200 in the early 20th century and then decreased. Dorje Pagmo is said to be the incarnation of the female tantric deity Vajravarahi, the Adamantine Sow. She enjoyed great respect among Buddhists. The bodies of her former incarnations have been preserved in the monastery. Samding was originally a small monastery but it was expanded by the fifth Dorje Pagmo.

Gyirong Phagpa Lhakhang (Gyirong County, Shigatse Prefecture)

The temple Gyirong Phagpa Lhakhang is in Gyirong County in Shigatse Prefecture. It was built in the style of a Nepalese monastery by Songtsen Gampo, at the proposal of his Nepalese queen. Therefore, it is more than a thousand years old.

Phagpa Lhakhang looks like a pagoda made of stone and wood. It consists of four stories, which are connected by staircases inside. Each story has a small door and windows. The higher the story, the smaller it is. The ground floor has a prayer hall, the main section of the *lhakhang* (temple). As well as the hall itself, there is a porch and interior and exterior corridors used for circumambulation. South of the hall are nine rooms, originally monks' quarters.

Judging by its murals, the temple seems to have been repaired several times. Its main section still has its original South Asian style. The style and content of the murals indicate that the early paintings in the lower section date back to the Tubo period, contemporary with or later than the time when the temple itself was built. The later paintings may be divided into two groups – those in the upper part of the eastern wall's southern section, which were done in the 14th century, and the paintings in the upper part of the eastern wall's northern section, which were done after the 15th century. The paintings reflect the important periods during which the temple was repaired.

No monks live in the temple any more and a caretaker is now in charge.

Chapter 6

The Potala Palace

Tibet, a Politico-Religious Regime under Central Government Rule

Having put Tibet under his control, Gushri Khan founded the Ganden Potrang regime in collaboration with the Gelugpa sect. He became the ruler of all Tibetan-inhabited areas, being the khan of all the Tibetan areas in Gansu, Qinghai and Kham as well as in Ü-Tsang. He sent his eight sons to station troops in Qinghai, where he established the base area of the Hoshot Mongols under his leadership. He ordered that the tax revenue from Kham be given to the Qinghai troops and that the tax revenue from Ü-Tsang be given to the Dalai and Panchen Lamas, so that the Gelugpa sect's monasteries got a lot of economic benefit. He and his two sons personally attended to garrison duties in Lhasa. His troops that were stationed in Dam (now Damxung), north of Lhasa, played a threatening and protective role. He thus consolidated his rule over Tibet. Tibetan high-ranking officials and secular aristocrats in the Ganden Potrang regime were appointed and granted honorific titles by Gushri Khan. The highest-ranking official was the Depa (chief administrator). Administrative orders for Ü-Tsang had to be issued and sealed by Gushri Khan. Decrees for the orders had to be sealed first by Gushri

Khan and then countersigned by the Depa.

A Qing government had been set up in northeast China, and Gushri Khan sensed that Ming rule was tottering and that it would not take long for the Qing government to occupy central China. Therefore, when Gushri Khan occupied Qinghai, he decided to seek the support of the Manchus. He suggested to the fifth Dalai Lama and the fourth Panchen Lama that a goodwill mission be sent to meet the Qing emperor. After consultation with the Depa, the Dalai and Panchen Lamas decided to send a mission headed by Ila Kuksan (also known as Sechen Chogyel) to Mukden (now Shenyang in Liaoning Province). The mission arrived in Mukden in 1642 and was greeted by Emperor Taizong outside the city walls. The warm reception showed that the Qing rulers attached great importance to the support of the Tibetans and Mongols. Emperor Taizong presented the mission with many gifts. The following year, the emperor sent envoys to accompany Ila Kuksan to Tibet. Ila Kuksan returned to Tibet with autographed letters and gifts from Emperor Taizong for Gushri Khan, the Dalai Lama, the Panchen Lama, Desi Tsangpa and other political and religious leaders of Tibet.

After Emperor Shunzhi ascended the throne in Beijing in 1644, the Qing court made more contact with Tibet. The following year, Gushri Khan

A fresco showing the fifth Dalai Lama being received by the Qing Emperor Shunzhi.

sent his son Dorje Dalai Batur Teji as envoy to Beijing with a letter for the emperor, in which he declared his allegiance to the Qing government. In addition, Gushri Khan and the fifth Dalai Lama sent a joint delegation to Beijing, which paid homage to the court and offered local Tibetan products to the emperor as gifts. The emperor gave the delegation gifts in return. From then on, Gushri Khan and the Dalai and Panchen Lamas sent envoys to Beijing nearly every year to offer tribute, and the Qing court gave them gifts in return.

To strengthen ties with the central government, Gushri Khan sent a letter to the emperor to ask him to invite the fifth Dalai Lama to Beijing. He said: "The Dalai Lama has achieved great merit. Please invite him to the capital city to chant sutras and give sermons, and this will bring benefit and fortune." At the same time, he urged the fifth Dalai Lama to accept the

A silver statue of the fifth Dalai Lama given to the Qing Emperor by the fifth Dalai Lama in 1652.

emperor's invitation. In 1652 (the ninth year of Shunzhi's reign), the Dalai Lama left for Beijing with a large entourage. He was greeted by the emperor in Nanyuan in the capital's southern suburbs while the emperor was on a "hunting trip." In the capital, the emperor gave a banquet in the Dalai Lama's honor and gave him large quantities of gold, silver, brocade, jewels, and jade articles as gifts. The Dalai Lama offered coral, jade, *phrug* (tweed), horses and lambskin in tribute to the emperor. During the Dalai Lama's two-month

A gold seal of authority bestowed by the Qing emperor on the fifth Panchen Lama.

stay in Beijing, Emperor Shunzhi and the Manchu and Mongol princes held banquets in his honor in turn. The Dalai Lama carried out Buddhist activities for them, including a sermon he gave specially to the Mongol prince Horchin Bintu, who had traveled from Mongolia, and Han monks who had come from Mount Wutai in Shanxi Province. The Dalai Lama stayed in the Yellow Temple (Huang Si), which had been specially built for him. Numerous gifts were bestowed on him. In early 1653, the Dalai Lama begged to return home. The emperor then provided him with an escort of Manchu soldiers to accompany him to Taike (now Liangcheng in Inner Mongolia). In Taike, the Dalai Lama received a gold album conferring a title on him and a gold seal of authority from the emperor. The gold seal bore the inscription "Seal of the Dalai Lama, Buddha of Great Compassion in the West, Leader of the Buddhist Faith Beneath the Sky, Holder of the Vajra." Through the album and seal, the Qing court gave official recognition to the Dalai Lama as religious leader in Tibetan and Mongolian areas, and the system of appointing successive Dalai Lamas by the Qing court was established. While the emperor granted this title to the Dalai Lama, he also conferred a title on Gushri Khan with a gold album and gold seal of authority. The seal's inscription read "Seal of the Righteous and Wise Gushri Khan," written in the Chinese, Manchu and Tibetan languages. Gushri Khan's status as ruler of Tibet was officially recognized by the Qing court through the album and seal. Qing support played an important role in strengthening the newly established Ganden Potrang regime.

Gushri Khan died in 1654. His sons fought for the throne for four years and finally came to a compromise. The Hoshot tribe in Qinghai was put under the rule of Tashi Batur, while Tibet came under Dayan Khan. However, Gushri Khan's sons did not enjoy the prestige of their father. At the same time, the support of the Qing court meant that the fifth Dalai Lama's prestige increased every day. In 1658, Depa Sonam Rabten, who had been appointed by Gushri Khan, died. After two years of consultation, the fifth Dalai Lama appointed his follower Drongmepai Trinley Gyatso as the new Depa. From that time on, the Dalai Lama rather than the Mongol khan had the power to appoint the Depa. After the fourth Panchen Lama, Lozang Choskyi Gyaltsen, died in 1662, the Dalai Lama accumulated more and more political and religious power. But the Gelugpa sect still relied on the Mongol Hoshot tribe for military protection. Dayan Khan died in 1668 and the khan's throne was vacant for three years until 1671, when Dalai Khan came to the throne.

In 1676, the fifth Dalai Lama proposed the appointment of Sangye Gyatso as Depa. Sangye Gyatso was then only 24 years old. He refused the appointment because he sensed that the conditions were not ripe. The Dalai Lama had to appoint Lozang Jinpa, his *chopon* (monk in charge of sacrificial offerings), as Depa. It was decided beforehand that Lozang Jinpa should resign his position after three years. In 1679, the Dalai Lama appointed Sangye Gyatso, who then officially assumed the post of Depa. In 1682, the fifth Dalai Lama died. Sangye Gyatso, in an attempt to monopolize power, kept secret the news of the death. He continued to exercise power in the name of the Dalai Lama. Sangye Gyatso sensed that Qing support was necessary for him to be a ruler of Tibet in both theory and practice. In 1694, the 33rd year of the Qing Emperor Kangxi's reign,

Sangye Gyatso presented the emperor with a forged letter purportedly from the Dalai Lama, saying that the Dalai Lama, "because of senility, has left all his government responsibilities to the Depa, so the Depa needs an honorific title." The Qing emperor complied, granting Sangye Gyatso the title Lord of Dharma. To stop his power being taken away by the Hoshot tribe, Sangye Gyatso colluded with Galdan, a chieftain of the Dzungar Mongols of Xinjiang, and used the conflicts between the Dzungar and Hoshot tribes to put down the Hoshot. In 1693, Sangye Gyatso, in the name of the fifth Dalai Lama, had spoken in defense of Galdan when the latter was in conflict with the Qing court, and Emperor Kangxi severely rebuked Sangye Gyatso. Sangye Gyatso put the search for the fifth Dalai Lama's reincarnation under his control. In 1685, he secretly confirmed that Tsangyang Gyatso, who was born in Monyul, was the Dalai Lama's reincarnation. It was not until 1694, when Qing troops defeated Galdan, that Emperor Kangxi learned from the captured enemy soldiers that the fifth Dalai Lama had been dead for a long time. The emperor wrote to Sangye Gyatso, denouncing him in stern language. By this time, Sangye Gyatso had sent a memorial to the emperor, saying that the Dalai Lama had died many years before and that his reincarnation had been identified. The Qing court approved the confirmation of Tsangyang Gyatso as Dalai Lama. In 1697, Tsangyang Gyatso was taken to Lhasa. En route to Lhasa, he met Lozang Yeshe, the fifth Panchen Lama, in Nankartse Dzong in Tsang. Lozang Yeshe shaved Tsangyang Gyatso's head and administered his vows as a monk. Then Tsangyang Gyatso was enthroned in the Potala.

After the fifth Dalai Lama died, the relationship between the new khan and Depa Sangye Gyatso began to sour. Sangye Gyatso tried in vain to strengthen his power through political plots. His support for the Dzungar Mongols brought him bad relations with the Qing court. In 1701, Dalai Khan died and Lhazang Khan ascended the throne. The power struggle between Sangye Gyatso and the khan grew worse. In 1703, the contradiction between them was mitigated temporarily through the mediation of high-ranking monks from Lhasa's three great monasteries. The khan and the Depa reached a compromise. Sangye Gyatso resigned as Depa, to be succeeded by his son Drosa. Lhazang Khan moved to Damxung. However, the compromise did not last long. In 1705, Sangye Gyatso assembled his militia in Ü-Tsang in a bid to drive Lhazang Khan out of Tibet. At the same time, the khan secretly called in his cavalry from Damxung. War broke out in Phanpo between the Depa and the Mongol khan. It ended in the defeat of the Tibetan troops and the capture and putting to death of Sangye Gyatso.

After the war, Lhazang Khan sent men to Beijing to report to the emperor about the former Depa's conspiracy and to ask the emperor to dethrone Tsangyang Gyatso on the grounds that he had indulged in sensual pleasures and had no regard for Buddhist discipline. In response, the emperor sent the military commander Xi Zhu and Chancellor Shu Lan to Tibet on a mission to placate Lhazang Khan, whom the emperor granted the honorific title of Supporter of the Doctrine, the Obedient Khan. The emperor ordered that the "sham Dalai Lama" Tsangyang Gyatso and Sangye Gyatso's wife and sons be brought to the capital in captivity. Tsangyang Gyatso died on the way to Beijing at the age of 24. After Tsangyang Gyatso had left for Beijing, Lhazang Khan installed Yeshe Gyatso as the sixth Dalai Lama. The Qing court approved this appointment in 1707 and conferred a gold seal of authority on Yeshe Gyatso in 1709. Yeshe Gyatso was enthroned as the sixth Dalai Lama in the Potala. The fifth Panchen Lama presided over the enthronement ceremony.

Nevertheless, the new Dalai Lama installed by Lhazang Khan was not acceptable to the monks of the three major monasteries or to the Hoshot tribe's aristocrats in Qinghai, who were dissatisfied with Lhazang

Khan. There was an air of unrest in Tibet. The high-ranking lamas of the three major monasteries secretly sent men to search for Tsangyang Gyatso's reincarnation in Litang, using as a clue a poem written by Tsangyang Gyatso: "Oh, white crane flying in the sky, please lend me your wings. I will not fly far away. I'll fly to Litang for a while and then come back." In about 1708, they found Kelzang Gyatso, who had been born in Litang (in what is now Sichuan Province) earlier in 1708. They regarded Kelzang Gyatso as Tsangyang Gyatso's reincarnation and sent him to Dêgê for protection. It was difficult for the Qing court to handle the affair, so the court ordered them to escort Kelzang Gyatso to Kumbum Monastery.

Worried about Lhazang Khan's discord with Qinghai's Mongol leaders, Emperor Kangxi sent Vice-Minister He Shou to Tibet to "assist Lhazang Khan in handling Tibetan affairs."

Just as the emperor suspected, Tsewang Rabten, a chieftain of the Dzungar tribe in Xinjiang, had taken advantage of the political unrest. Tsewang Rabten confused Lhazang Khan by arranging for the khan's son to marry Tsewang Rabten's daughter. Then, on the pretext of escorting his daughter and son-in-law, he suddenly attacked Tibet. Meanwhile, he also sent troops to Kumbum Monastery to capture Kelzang Gyatso. It was not until Dzungar troops reached northern Tibet that Lhazang Khan began to realize what a bad situation it was. He hurriedly gathered his men to resist. Though the Dzungar troops sent to Kumbum were defeated by Qing troops, those who had reached northern Tibet still declared that they would escort the "true" Dalai Lama to Lhasa, attempting to sap the will to fight among Lhazang Khan's soldiers. The war was not settled. Lhazang Khan hurriedly retreated to Lhasa to defend the city until Qing reinforcements could arrive. With the help of lay and religious people who were dissatisfied with Lhazang Khan, Dzungar troops eventually stormed into Lhasa. Lhazang Khan hid in the Potala but was soon killed by enemy troops when he tried to break out of their encirclement. The Dzungars occupied Lhasa, deposed Yeshe Gyatso, and appointed officials. They committed arson, killed, and pillaged. Many monasteries in Lhasa including Chokhorgyal and Mindroling monasteries, were ransacked after their monks refused to surrender. Those who had pinned their hopes on the Dzungar troops were disappointed.

In 1718, the Qing court ordered western Mongolian Elute generals from Xi'an to lead an army of several thousand men into Tibet. The Qing troops were eventually annihilated when they ran out of food. The tragic defeat of the Qing troops in Tibet gave rise to debate among princes and ministers in Beijing. But Emperor Kangxi said that Tibet was the shield of Qinghai, Yunnan and Sichuan and that its seizure by the Dzungar Mongols would mean there would be no peace at the border. Therefore, it was decided to launch a military expedition. A second military campaign was organized in 1720. That same year, the emperor confirmed Kelzang Gyatso as the reincarnation of the sixth Dalai Lama and ordered him to be taken to Lhasa to be enthroned. The Qing court again sent troops to Tibet to fight the Mongol invaders. Led by the Lhazang Khan administration officials Khangchenne and Pholhanas, Tibetans attacked enemy-occupied Lhasa from Ngari and Shigatse in Tsang. Meanwhile, two other officials of the old government, Ngabopa and Jaranas, organized a people's force in Ü in co-ordination with Qing troops. Facing such strongly armed Qing troops, the Dzungar invaders fled after putting up little resistance. There were 7,000 Dzungar troops at the beginning of the battle but only 1,000 of them could flee back to Dzungar.

After driving away the Dzungar troops, the Qing court put the administration of Tibet under the direct control of the Qing central government rather than the Qinghai Mongol chieftains. The emperor appointed some Tibetan aristocrats *kalons* (ministers of the Tibetan government), headed by Khangchenne. However, a power struggle broke out in 1727 among the *kalons*. Ngabopa, in collaboration with the *kalons* Lumpanas and Jaranas, murdered Khangchenne, the chief *kalon*, and sent men to Tsang to capture the *kalon* Pholhanas. Pholhanas reported on the rebellion to the Qing court and launched a punitive expedition from Tsang. With several thousand men that he gathered in Tsang and with the help of Gashinas, the chief administrator of Ngari and the brother of Khangchenne, Pholhanas occupied Lhasa after a six-month battle with Ngabopa. With the help of the monks of the three major monasteries, he captured Ngabopa, Lumpanas and Jaranas in 1728. He put the three rival *kalons* under house arrest and waited for the Qing court's instructions. Learning of the internecine strife in Tibet, the Qing court sent armed forces to the area to help restore peace and order. When the Qing army arrived in Lhasa, Pholhanas formed a court of justice with Qing officials. The

A fresco of Pholhanas in Sera Monastery.

court put to death Ngabopa and other rebels, and the violent incident was brought to an end. In recognition of Pholhanas' contribution to ending the turmoil, the Qing emperor conferred on him the title of *beizi* (a Manchu hereditary title) and appointed him chief *kalon*. The emperor later conferred on him the title of prince and made him chief administrator of Tibet.

To protect Tibet from a Dzungar invasion, Emperor Yongzheng ordered the seventh Dalai Lama to be taken to Huiyuan Monastery in Taining, Sichuan Province. The emperor ordered the Dalai Lama's father to go to

A gold statue of Sakyamuni offered to the Qing court by Pholhanas and the seventh Dalai Lama as a tribute in 1745.

Beijing and made him a lord to guard against his interfering in Tibet's political affairs. This was the beginning of the Dalai Lama's relatives being granted honorific titles. It was not until 1735, when the Dzungars were no longer a threat to Tibet, that the Dalai Lama was escorted back to Lhasa. In 1727, to keep a close watch on the Tibetan leaders, the Qing government created the office of *ambans* (Qing ministers who lived in the territory of a tributary state or dependency). The Qing authorities built a garrison of 2,000 men under the command of Tibet's *ambans* to maintain law and order. The Qing government delimited the border between Tibet on the one hand and Qinghai, Sichuan and Yunnan on the other to establish Tibet's administrative area.

Pholhanas helped stabilize society after the war, improve living standards, and strengthen Tibet's military. Following the example of the Qing troops stationed in Tibet, he trained a Tibetan garrison of 10,000 cavalrymen and 15,000 foot soldiers, so that Tibet had a well-trained and well-equipped army. He set up checkpoints along the roads between Tibet and the Dzungar tribal area to defend Tibet against a Dzungar invasion. He made improvements to post stations to guarantee the transmission of official documents.

Pholhanas died in 1747. His son Gyumey Namgyel inherited his father's title of prince and became Tibet's chief administrator. The new prince was domineering and despotic. He formed a clique to pursue his selfish interests, murdered his brother, the administrator of Ngari, and was on bad terms with the Dalai Lama. He became very hostile to the *ambans*. He cut off the transmission of government documents and tried to win the support of the Dzungars. A large proportion of the Qing troops stationed in Tibet had been sent back in 1733, so the situation of Tibet became critical. The ambans Fu Qing and Labdon took pre-emptive action to kill Gyumey Namgyel. When Gyumey Namgyel's men later killed Fu Qing and Labdon, chaos reigned in Tibet for a short period of time. The offices of the *ambans* were burnt and robbed in what became known as the Gyumey Namgyel rebellion.

Soon after the rebellion, the seventh Dalai Lama appointed Doring Pandita as Tibet's acting chief administrator and had the murderers of the *ambans* captured as he waited for Qing officials to deal with the matter. The emperor sent Celeng, the governor of Sichuan, into Tibet with troops to restore order. After studying all aspects of the Tibet issue, Celeng produced a 13-point "program for the new administration of Tibet."

After examining the Qing Dynasty's former policy on Tibet, Emperor Qianlong decided to take advantage of the incident to make changes to Tibet's administrative structure. The Qing court rescinded the post of prince and created the administrative structure of the Kashag, the Tibetan local government. The Kashag consisted of four *kalons* (ministers) – one monk and three laymen, who jointly took charge of local Tibetan affairs. This was the first time that a monk had been appointed a *kalon*. The *kalons* had to obtain the approval of the *ambans* and Dalai Lama on important issues. Minor matters were left to the discretion of the *kalons* under the supervision of the *ambans*.

The seventh Dalai Lama died in 1757. The emperor appointed Demo Nomihan regent to act in the Dalai Lama's place. This marked the inception of a regency in Tibet. The Qing court sent Changkya Hutuktu to search for the reincarnation of the seventh Dalai Lama. Changkya Hutuktu and the sixth Panchen Lama found Jampel Gyatso, who was confirmed as the reincarnation. Jampel Gyatso (1758-1804) became the eighth Dalai Lama.

The regent Demo Nomihan died in 1777 and, by order of the emperor, was succeeded by the Tsemonling Hutuktu, the abbot of Beijing's Yonghe Gong (Lamasery of Harmony and Peace). A system was set up at this time whereby the Dalai Lama, *ambans* and regent would jointly adminis-

A *tangka* of White Manjushri, given in tribute to the Qing emperor by the sixth Panchen Lama.

ter Tibet. In 1779, the Qing court invited the sixth Panchen Lama to Beijing. The Panchen Lama arrived in Rehe in August 1780 to attend the Qing Emperor Qianlong's 70th birthday celebrations. The Panchen Lama then went to Beijing. He died in late October in Beijing's Yellow Temple (Huang Si). In 1784, the eighth Dalai Lama assumed office. The Changkya Hutuktu, Rolpai Dorje, died in 1786. By order of the Qing court, Tsemonling returned to Beijing, and the Jedrung Hutuktu was named Tsemonling's successor as the Dalai Lama's assistant in the administration of Tibet.

In 1788, the Gurkhas invaded the Tsang region of Tibet. Tsang bordered the Gurkha area, so the Tibetans and Gurkhas had close economic ties, engaging in barter and other trade. However, a serious dispute arose between the Tibetans and Gurkhas. In 1788, using the pretext that Tibet had increased the duties levied on Gurkha goods in the border region, 3,000 Gurkha troops occupied Kyirong, Nyalam and Dzongkhar. The Qing Emperor Qianlong dispatched troops under the joint command of General Ehui of

A *tangka* of the sixth Panchen Lama.

Chengdu and General Cheng De, the Sichuan garrison commander, to drive the invaders out of Tibet. The emperor dispatched Bazhong, deputy chairman of the Board for National Minority Affairs, as imperial envoy to Tibet to investigate and handle the affair together with Ehui and Cheng De. Before Bazhong arrived in Tibet, the Drungpa Hutuktu of Tsang had privately made peace with the Gurkhas and promised to redeem the lost land by giving them money. After arriving in Lhasa, Bazhong consulted with Ehui and Cheng De and then ordered the Shamar Tulku (Red Hat) to inform the Gurkhas to surrender and withdraw from the territory they had occupied. Meanwhile, through his own representative, Bazhong negotiated terms with the Gurkhas for their withdrawal. It was agreed that the Gurkhas would leave the territory they had occupied and that they were to be guaranteed a payment of 300 silver ingots each year as compensation. In a report to the emperor, Bazhong said: "Nyalam, Dzongkhar and Kyirong have been recovered." He then asked to be allowed to "return with the victorious army." In 1790, when the Gurkhas asked Tibet to honor the compensation agreement, the Dalai Lama and the Kashag refused and asked the Gurkhas to cancel the agreement. However, the Gurkhas refused. This was reported to the Qing court. It was not until then that the Qing court realized that the "victory" that Bazhong reported was not a real one.

Due to the critical situation in Tibet, the Qing court again sent Tsemonling there to act as regent. He died in March 1791, several months after arriving in Lhasa. The Qing court sent the eighth Jedrung Hutuktu to be regent.

Using the pretext that the Tibetans had not honored the agreement, the Gurkhas invaded Tibet for a second time in July 1791, reoccupying Nyalam, Dingri, Sakya and Kyirong in 10 days or so. The Shamar Tulku, stepbrother of both the sixth Panchen Lama and of the Drungpa Hutuktu, wanted to take revenge on the Drungpa Hutuktu for not having shared the wealth left by the sixth Panchen Lama, so the Shamar Tulku secretly went to the Gurkhas and told their ruler that it was then the best time for them to take possession of the treasures in Tashilhunpo Monastery. As the Gurkhas were advancing to Tashilhunpo, Amban Baotai in alarm moved the seventh Panchen Lama from Tashilhunpo to Lhasa. The Panchen Lama was thus saved from capture by the Gurkhas. The Drungpa Hutuktu fled with some valuables. The monks, the Tashilhunpo's Jedrung Lama and a *dratsang khenpo* (head of a *dratsang* or college) went into hiding, having been frightened by an oracle who had warned against any resistance to the invaders. The Gurkha invaders plundered Tashilhunpo Monastery of all its treasures. The only resistance came from 80 Qing garrison troops under the command of a low-ranking officer called Xu Nanpeng, who held out for several days and nights in the Shigatse fort. The Qing court was shocked by the news of the foreign invasion. Bazhong committed suicide by drowning himself in a lake to escape punishment. The Qing court promptly sent to Tibet a large force of 17,000 troops under the command of Fukang'an, whom the emperor appointed commander-in-chief, and Hai Lancha, the consultant minister. They were ordered to enter Tibet along three routes. With the support of the Tibetan people, the Qing troops soon regained all the territory occupied by the Gurkhas and drove all the Gurkha invaders out of Tibet by May 1792. The Qing troops later marched into Gurkha territory in July and were only 20 *li* (10 kilometers) from Yambu (Kathmandu), the Gurkha capital. The Gurkha ruler, seeing that there was no way out, sent a chieftain to announce their surrender. The ruler returned all the Tashilhunpo treasures and the Panchen Lama's gold album that they had looted. In a written statement, the Gurkha ruler pledged never again to invade Tibet, and he promised to send his chieftain to Beijing to offer a humble apology and to pay tribute. Emperor Qianlong had given instructions that the army must withdraw before any heavy snow, so Fukang'an granted the Gurkha ruler's appeal for peace. In September, Fukang'an returned to Tibet with the victori-

The "Imperial Ordinance for the More Effective Governance of Tibet."

ous army.

On the instructions of Emperor Qianlong1792-1793, Fukang'an, together with Sun Shiyi, Hui Ling and *ambans* He Ling, worked out regulations to reform Tibet's administration, including the 29-article "Imperial Ordinance for the More Effective Governance of Tibet."

The Imperial Ordinance was an important legal document that the Qing dynasty drew up to exercise sovereignty over Tibet, on the basis of the Yuan and Ming dynasties' experiences of administering Tibet. The ordinance showed that Qing administration of Tibet had matured. The implementation of the ordinance played a positive role in developing the central government's ties with Tibet and good relations between the national minorities, consolidating the defense of the southwestern border, protecting Tibet from foreign invasion, promoting production, and improving the Tibetan people's basic living conditions.

In 1804, the eighth Dalai Lama died. Following his death, the Jedrung

After defeating the Gurkha invasion of 1792, Emperor Qianlong stipulated that the candidates for the Dalai Lama, Panchen Lama and other great incarnate lamas be determined by the drawing of lots from a golden urn before the statue of Sakyamuni in the Jokhang Temple. During the Qing dynasty, three Dalai Lamas, two Panchen Lamas and dozens of other incarnate lamas were determined by the drawing of lots from the golden urn.

Hutuktu was appointed regent by Emperor Jiaqing. In 1807, in a joint request to the *amban*, the Jedrung Hutuktu, as well as monks and lay Tibetan people, said that the boy they had found in Danko in Sichuan was the genuine reincarnation of the eighth Dalai Lama, so they were seeking the emperor's permission to dispense with the system of drawing lots from a golden urn. The emperor approved the request. The ninth Dalai Lama, Lungtok Gyatso, was enthroned at the Potala Palace in 1815.

The regent Jedrung Hutuktu died in 1811. The Qing court installed the eighth Demo Hutuktu as regent. In 1815, the ninth Dalai Lama died at the age of just 10.

In 1818, the regent requested, through the *amban*, that Emperor Jiaqing recognize as the reincarnation of the ninth Dalai Lama the boy that the regent found in Litang and to exempt the regent from drawing lots from the golden urn. The regent's request was refused and the *amban* was criticized. On the emperor's orders, two other boys were selected as candidates for the reincarnation, so there were three claimants to the Dalai Lama's throne. In 1822, the three were brought to Lhasa as ordered by the emperor, and the drawing of lots from the golden urn established the Litang boy Tsultrim Gyatso

The gold-leaf album from the Qing emperor conferring on its recipient the title of the 11th Dalai Lama.

The Potala.

(1816-37) as the 10th Dalai Lama. Tsultrim Gyatso was enthroned accordingly.

The eighth Demo Hutuktu died in 1818. The Qing court ordered the second Tsemonling Hutuktu, who was born in Gannan (southern Gansu) and was abbot of Beijing's Yonghe Gong, to be regent.

In 1830, *amban* Xing Ke, together with the 10th Dalai Lama and the regent, sent Kalon Shatra and other people to assess the number of households and residents in Tibet and the amount collected as corvée and tax from the *dzongs* (counties) and *shikas* (villages). An inventory was made and submitted to and approved by the *amban* and the Dalai Lama. This was the largest survey of land, corvée and taxes in Tibet conducted by the Qing court. In 1837, the 10th Dalai Lama died. The regent Tsemonling Hutuktu was responsible for searching for the Dalai Lama's reincarnation. In 1841, the drawing of lots from the golden urn confirmed Khedrup Gyatso (1838-55) to be the 11th Dalai Lama. In the same year, Tibet's troops and people defeated Senpa invaders who were supported by Great Britain. This was another victory over foreign invaders achieved by the Tibetan people under the guidance of the *amban*, following the counterattacks against the two Gurkha invasions.

During the Qing Dynasty, Tibet was ruled by the central government. On the one hand, the central government tightened its control of Tibet, reformed the region's political system, set up new political institutions, and installed the amban, the Qing's resident minister in Tibet, who was responsible for handling Tibet's affairs on behalf of the central government. On the other hand, Tibet's system of feudal serfdom developed further, characterized by a merging of secular political and religious rule. Under this politico-religious rule, the ruling cliques of the monasteries gradually took control of all aspects of life in Tibet. The economy of the monasteries made up a large part of Tibet's overall economy. Monastery buildings still constitute the major cultural sites from this period. Some buildings, such as the Potala Palace, were built on a large scale and finally came to fruition during the Qing Dynasty, even though they were founded years before.

Potala Palace (Lhasa)

The Potala Palace is located on Lhasa's Potala Hill. Potala is a Sanskrit word and is the name of the paradise island of the deity Avalokiteshvara.

The Potala is a huge and magnificent complex of ancient buildings. It was built in a specific Tibetan style characterized by a traditional Tibetan blockhouse of wood and stone, Han Chinese great halls, and Indian and Nepalese religious buildings. It is a symbol of Tibetan artistic achievement and cultural prosperity, and an art treasure on the roof of the world. The palace complex is one of China's cultural sites under state protection and is also on the UNESCO World Heritage List.

The first palace on the site was built by the Tubo king Songtsen Gampo in the seventh century AD. It was later destroyed by storms and war. Only the Dharma King Practice Chamber and the Lokeshvara Chapel remained. Construction of the present Potala began in the 17th century and was continued by successive Dalai Lamas. The Potala complex covers an area of 41 hectares. The main building is 360 meters long and 140 meters wide. It is 117.19 meters tall at its highest point and covers an area of nine hectares.

The Red Palace has many chapels, including halls housing the stupas of successive Dalai Lamas. The fifth Dalai Lama's stupa is the most exquisite. It stands in the west side of the Red Palace's fourth floor. Built in 1690, the stupa is 14.85 meters high, in five levels divided into a base, a middle section, and a top. The fifth Dalai Lama's body has been preserved with perfume and safflower in the middle section. The stupa is covered with 3,724 kilograms of gold leaf and 15,000 diamonds,

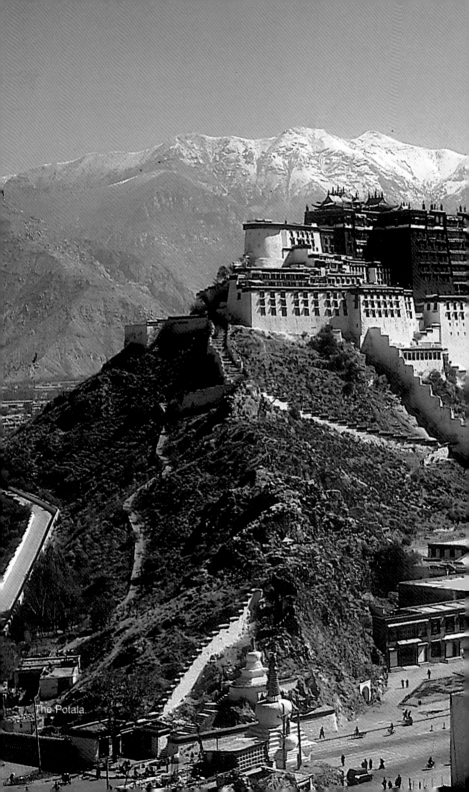

The Potala.

jade pieces, pearls and agate pieces. On the stupa's base are gold lamps and bowls, enamel and porcelain objects from the Ming and Qing dynasties, and various religious objects, as well as eight silver Buddhist pagodas on two sides. The top of the stupa is made of gold and dazzles brilliantly.

East of the stupa chapel is the Sishi Phuntsok Hall, the Red Palace's largest hall. The hall covers an area of 700 square meters and has a ceiling six meters high. Forty-eight solid pillars support the roof. The pillars and *dougong* set of brackets are square. The beams are decorated with paintings, lion and tiger patterns, and wooden images of Buddha. In the chapel is a horizontal tablet given by the Qing Emperor Qianlong, which bears the Chinese characters "Yong lian chu chi" (holy spot of the emerging lotus). There are paintings above the door lintel, on the walls and in the corridors, the best-known being "The fifth Dalai Lama having an audience with the Qing Emperor Shunzhi in Beijing in 1652."

The golden roof of the Potala.

Second only to the fifth Dalai Lama's stupa is the stupa of the 13th Dalai Lama, Thubten Gyatso. It is as large and splendid as that of the fifth Dalai Lama. It is the most valuable of the eight stupas. Built in 1936, it is the Red Palace's highest structure at 14 meters tall. It is decorated with 590 kilograms of gold, as well as diamonds, pearls, turquoise, coral, agate and other jewels. The most beautiful piece of furniture is a pearl pagoda (mandala) decorated with pearls and coral connected by golden thread. Some of the murals relate events in the Dalai Lama's life and his audience with Empress Dowager Cixi and Emperor Guangxu in 1908.

The entrance to the Potala's Eastern Hall.

The White Palace contains the private quarters of successive Dalai Lamas, as well as offices of the Kashag, Tibet's former local government. The Eastern Audience Hall (Tsogchen Shar) was the White Palace's main building. It has 30 pillars and covers an area of 500 square meters. It was where the Dalai Lama was enthroned and where important religious and political activities were held. On the top floor of the White Palace are two bedrooms: the western one is called the Western Sunlight Room and the eastern one the Eastern Sunlight Room. The Dalai Lama lived here and engaged in political and religious activities.

East of the White Palace is the inner courtyard known as the Deyangshar, which has an area of 1,600 square meters. A grand religious dance would be held here every year on the 29th day of the 12th month of the Tibetan lunar calendar. On that day, the Dalai Lama would enjoy the performance from the Eastern Sunlight Room together with high-ranking monks and lay officials of the Kashag government. The residents of Lhasa could also come to watch the dance. The courtyard would be full of people and there would be a lively atmosphere on that day.

The Sasum Namgyal (Hall Celebrating Victory over the Three Worlds) is in the very middle of the Red Palace's top story. It has a painting of Emperor Qianlong and a tablet that says, "Long live the emperor" in Chinese. It was an important chapel, where the *amban* and the Kashag held important activities, such as drawing lots from the golden urn (in the ceremony to confirm the Dalai Lama's reincarnation).

The Chogyel Drupug (Dharma King Practice Chamber) is one of the oldest rooms in the Potala. Songtsen Gampo is said to have used this dark, small cell as his meditation chamber. It is now filled with statues of Songtsen Gampo, Princess Wencheng and Princess Bhrikuti Devi (Tritsun), as well as of the ministers Gar Tongtsen and Thonmi Sambhota. The simple and vivid-looking statues are said to have been made at the time of Songtsen Gampo.

Above the Chogyel Drupug is the Lokeshvara Chapel (Phagpa Lhakhang). These two shrines are the oldest in the Potala, dating back to the seventh century and the time of Songtsen Gampo. Tibetans consider the Lokeshvara Chapel to be the holiest shrine in the Potala. The chapel is dedicated to Avalokiteshvara, one of whose titles is Lokeshvara. Hanging over the door is a large inscription given by the Qing Emperor Tongzhi, which reads, "Amazing fruits of the field of merit."

The Potala is renowned not only for its buildings but also for its works of art and precious cultural relics. As well as numerous statues and murals, it has a great number of sutras, particularly *Kangyur* of the Tibetan *Tripitaka* written in gold ink, and Indian sutras written on *pattra* leaves. There are also golden albums and seals of authority granted by emperors to the Dalai Lamas. The Potala may be regarded as an art museum and precious storehouse of culture and it is of great value for the study of Tibetan politics, economics, history, culture and art.

Norbulingka (Lhasa)

The Norbulingka, meaning "Jewel Park," is in the suburbs of Lhasa. The seventh Dalai Lama gave it its name, and successive Dalai Lamas used it as a summer residence and recreation area. The seventh Dalai Lama and succeeding Dalai Lamas would move from the Potala to the Norbulingka every sum-

The Norbulingka.

mer to handle government affairs there. The Norbulingka has now become a park open to the outside world. The seventh Dalai Lama constructed the first building here in the middle of the 18th century. The construction of the present Norbulingka was ascribed to succeeding Dalai Lamas and *ambans* in Tibet.

The shrine in the Dalai Lama's reception hall in the Norbulingka.

The Norbulingka contains a number of buildings and a big garden, occupying a total area of 360,000 square meters. The buildings include the Uru Potrang built by the *amban* for the seventh Dalai Lama; the Kelzang Potrang built by the seventh Dalai Lama; the Debating Platform, the Audience Hall, the artificial lake and its two shrines (the central shrine and the shrine dedicated to the Dragon King or Naga King) and the library, all built by the eighth Dalai Lama; and the Chensel Lingka, the Chensel Potrang, the Kelzang Dekyi Palace and the Tagtu Migyur Potrang, all built by the 13th Dalai Lama. The Kelzang Potrang, Chensel Potrang and Tagtu Migyur Potrang are the main buildings. Both the Kelzang Potrang and Chensel

Potrang have three stories, the ground floors being chanting halls, the middle floors containing the Dalai Lama's bedrooms, and the top floors containing chapels. The Tagtu Migyur Potrang is a two-story building. The bottom floor contains a small reception hall, while the upper floor contains the chanting hall and the Dalai Lama's chapel and bedroom. The Tagtu Migyur Potrang is well known for its beautiful murals. A detailed account of Tibetan history is painted on the walls.

The garden is full of trees and dotted with various beautiful flowers. It can be dated back to the period of the eighth Dalai Lama. The wooded areas and the buildings are in such harmony with each other that each adds its brilliance to the other. The beautiful lake and its two splendidly decorated shrines form a harmonious whole with their surroundings. The layout and formation of the garden reflect characteristics of those in Han areas. Here you will find a harmonious combination of buildings and a garden in Tibetan and Han styles.

Naga King (Dragon King) Pool (Lhasa)

The Naga King Pool.

The Naga King or Dragon King Pool is part of a small park in Lhasa. The pool is said to have been dedicated to the Naga King and eight dragons, whom the sixth Dalai Lama invited from Maizhokunggar to live there. It can be dated back to the period of the sixth Dalai Lama. After the fifth Dalai Lama had finished building the Potala's White Palace and Depa Sangye Gyatso had finished building its Red Palace, there was a large depression behind the Potala because of all the earth that had been removed to make mortar. The depression was filled with water and named the Dragon King Pool.

The pool is right behind the Potala. The pool's small park, with trees and paths, was built along the hillside. The pool is 270 meters long from east to west, and 112 meters long from north to south. There is a chapel on an island in the middle. The chapel is a square, mandalic building with three floors, facing south. The bottom floor is in the form of a regular cross and

Mindroling Monastery.

has a small chapel with four pillars, surrounded by corridors. The middle and top floors have chapels, the one on the top floor being a small, hexagonal chapel with a hexagonal pointed roof. Its regular structure and beautifully decorated carved beams and columns reflect a high level of artistic and building skill. The island is connected to the shore by an arched footbridge.

Mindroling Monastery (Dranang County in Shannan)

Mindroling Monastery was founded by Terdak Lingpa in 1676. He was a renowned teacher who had many disciples, one of whom was the fifth Dalai Lama. Mindroling is one of the largest and most important monasteries of the Nyingma sect in central Tibet. The post of its abbot was passed from father to son or son-in-law. It was burned to the ground in 1718 by Dzungar

Mindroling Monastery.

Mongols but was reconstructed by the seventh Dalai Lama. The monastery was again badly damaged in the 1960s during the Cultural Revolution but has been partially rebuilt. In the 1980s, it was opened to the outside world after renovation. It contains many silver, bronze, wooden and earthenware statues of Buddha, gilded stupas decorated with jewels, splendid small Buddhist pagodas, *tangka* paintings and many Buddhist documents.

Kwonti Lhakhang (Lhasa)

The temple Kwonti Lhakhang or Guandi Miao (dedicated to Guandi the god of war) is west of the Potala on Barmari Hill (also known as Millstone Hill because the top is as plain as a millstone). The main statue in the temple looks like Gesar, a legendary hero of Tibet, so the temple is also known as Gesar Lhakhang.

The temple was built in a Han style on the hillside, facing south. Just inside the entrance is a courtyard, which contains a pair of two-story buildings, one on the east and the other on the west. The ground floor of each was used as monks' quarters and the upper floor as a reception room and offices. In the north of the courtyard is the temple's main hall and the Hall of Manjushri.

A tablet stands in the courtyard. It gives an account of how Qing troops defeated Gurkha invaders in the 58th year of Emperor Qianlong's reign (1793) and how the monastery was founded. In the 56th year of Qianlong's reign (1791), when the Gurkhas again invaded Tibet, the Qing government sent troops under the command of General Fukang'an to Tibet. The Qing troops drove the invaders out of Tibet in the seventh lunar month of the 57th year of Qianlong's reign (1792). Qing troops built the temple on Millstone Hill at that time.

The temple's historical and cultural relics are important for the study of the Qing government's military affairs in Tibet. It is also a historical witness to how the Tibetan and Han people stood side by side to protect their sacred motherland against foreign invasion.

Chapter 7

Turbulent and Eventful Tibet

The second Tsemonling had been regent for more than 20 years and had great power. In 1844, the seventh Panchen Lama and some other high-ranking monks and officials feuded with the Tsemonling. Through the *amban*, Qi Shan, they impeached the regent before the emperor on charges of greed and graft, the exploitation of the common people, the murders of the ninth and 10th Dalai Lamas, and maltreatment of the 11th Dalai Lama. The emperor ordered that Tsemonling be removed from office and arrested. The monks of Sera Monastery tried to rescue the Tsemonling but failed. The Tsemonling was exiled to the region of Gannan (southern Gansu). Qi Shan then asked the seventh Panchen Lama to be acting regent. After acting as regent for seven months, the Panchen Lama resigned and went back to Tashilhunpo Monastery. The Qing court appointed the ninth Reting Hutuktu, Ngawang Yeshe Tsultrim Gyaltsen, as regent.

The high-ranking monks and officials were then always in discord with each other. In 1855, Reting Hutuktu and the *kalon* Shatra Wangchuk Gyalpo, through the *amban*, impeached Demo Hutuktu on a charge of violating Buddhist rules. The emperor ordered that Demo Hutuktu be imprisoned in Dzongkhar in Tsang. With the support of Britain, Nepal invaded Tsang in that year. The Tibetan people and troops bravely fought the invaders. The Qing government was busy suppressing the Taiping rebellion at that time. In 1856, under the direction of the *amban* Hetehe, the Tibetan local government signed an unequal treaty with Nepal, damaging Tibet's interests.

Not long afterward, the regent Reting Hutuktu and the *kalon* Shatra Wangchuk Gyalpo were in discord. Shatra Wangchuk Gyalpo unsuccessfully challenged the regent's power and was then himself removed from office and exiled from Lhasa to his estate in Nyêmo. Shatra's wife informed on him, saying he had secretly written to Nepalese officials. The regent ordered the Dapon Thonpa to punish Shatra. The Dapon sympathized with Shatra, had him confined to a monastery and forced him to become a monk.

In 1856 and 1858, the reincarnations of the eighth Panchen Lama and 12th Dalai Lama were confirmed through the drawing of lots from the golden urn. In early 1862, Shatra Wangchuk Gyalpo, together with some high-ranking monks from Ganden and Drepung monasteries, used the problem of almsgiving as an excuse to agitate monks at the two monasteries into staging a riot. The *amban* Man Qing took the side of the rioters. The regent, the Reting Hutuktu, fled from Lhasa to Beijing during the night, taking his official seals. The *amban* proposed to the emperor that Shatra Wangchuk Gyalpo be appointed as acting regent in charge of Shangshang. The Qing court approved the proposal and simultaneously sent officials to investigate and handle the matter. However, the problem was postponed for a long time due to bad communications and was eventually left unsolved. The Reting Hutuktu died in February 1863 and Shatra Wangchuk Gyalpo died in 1864. The struggle among the rulers ended without result.

The Qing court appointed Lozang Khenrab Wangchuk, a native of Tachienlu (now Kangding) in Sichuan and a lama who had been the sutra teacher of both the Ganden Tripa and Dalai Lama, as regent in 1866. The court granted him the title of Nominhan and he thus became the first Dedruk Hutuktu.

A fresco showing the Empress Dowager receiving the 13th Dalai Lama.

In 1871, Tibet experienced another rebellion. Palden Dondrup, the treasurer of Ganden Monastery who had helped Shatra Wangchuk Gyalpo assume power, incited some officials and monks of Ganden to kill some ecclesiastical and lay officials. He tried to force the regent, Dedruk Hutuktu, to resign and he tried to dethrone the 12th Dalai Lama. The regent and *amban* sent several thousand troops to attack Ganden Monastery. The defeated Palden Dondrup fled from Lhasa but was killed on the way.

The regent, Dedruk Hutuktu, died in 1872. The 12th Dalai Lama took over the reins of government upon coming of age but died within three months. The Qing court appointed the Jedrung Hutuktu, Ngawang Palden Chokyi Gyaltsen, as regent. Under his direction, the reincarnation of the 12th Dalai Lama was identified and confirmed as the 13th Dalai Lama by the drawing of lots from the golden urn. The eighth Panchen Lama died in August 1882 and the Jedrung Hutuktu died in 1886. The Qing court appointed the eighth Demo Hutuktu, Ngawang Lozang Trinley Rabgye, as regent. In 1888, the ninth Panchen Lama was confirmed by the drawing of lots from the golden urn. In 1894, the 13th Dalai Lama reached the age of 19, so the Demo Hutuktu resigned as regent, and the Dalai Lama took over the reins of government. The year 1899 saw a struggle against the 13th Dalai Lama by the former regent Demo Hutuktu and his trusted followers. The regent and his followers failed and were arrested. The Demo Hutuktu died in prison. Tengye Ling Monastery (in which Demo Hutuktu practiced Buddhism) and the Demo Hutuktu's estates, subsidiary monasteries and vassals were confiscated, and no search was allowed for the Demo Hutuktu's reincarnation.

After the Opium Wars, Britain, France and Russia took advantage of the unequal treaties they had signed with the Qing government and used the pretext of tourism to send explorers and missionaries into Tibetan-inhabited areas of China. Contending with Russia for hegemony in Asia, Britain expanded the sphere of its influence to the north of the Himalayas in order to consolidate its colonialist rule of India.

Faced with the expansion of British India, the Tibetan local government set up checkpoints in strategic passes along the Tibet-Sikkim border in 1884. A fortified checkpoint was built on Mount Lungthur in Renock Dzong, southwest of the pass Dzalep-la, to keep close watch on British-Indian activities in Sikkim. In 1885, Britain sent a mission through Sikkim to Tibet under the pretext of surveying Tibet's commerce and mineral deposits. Tibetan troops and civilians halted the mission. Under pressure from Britain, the Qing government ordered the garrison at Lungthur to withdraw. But the local Tibetan people refused to withdraw the garrison. The British eventually launched an attack on Mount Lungthur in February 1888. Because the Tibetan troops' weapons were far inferior to those of the British and because the Qing government made concessions and sought peace with the British invaders, the Tibetan people failed in their struggle against the British invasion. In February 1890, the Qing government signed the Convention Between Great Britain and China Relating to Sikkim and Tibet. This treaty forced the Qing government to recognize Sikkim's status as a British protectorate. Moreover, the British-proposed boundary at Dzalep-la between Sikkim and Tibet was imposed on China, depriving China of large tracts of pasturage as well as places of strategic importance from Renock Dzong to the south of Gampa Dzong.

In 1893, the British and the Qing government signed the Regulations Regarding Trade, Communication, and Pasturage to be Appended to the Sikkim-Tibet Convention of 1890. China agreed to establish a trade mart in Yadong open to all British subjects, who were able to enjoy extraterritorial rights. Moreover, China was to grant duty-free entry to British goods across the Sikkim-Tibet frontier for five years. The signing of the two treaties aroused great indignation among all the Chinese, including the Tibetan people.

In November 1903, the British government, under the pretext of escorting Francis Younghusband for an interview with the *amban*, sent an expeditionary army of 3,000 under the command of James Macdonald across the Dzalep-la pass. The invaders broke through the weakly defended Yadong-Phagri line and occupied Yadong. In July 1904, the British invaders defeated Tibetan troops in Samada Valley near Kangmar and occupied Gyangzê.

After the fall of Gyangzê, the British invaders pushed on to Lhasa. The struggle against the invasion took a drastic turn for the worse. The capitulationists gained the upper hand in the Tibetan local government. Under their pressure, the local government issued an order for the Tibetan army and people to cease their resistance. It sent high officials as peace negotiators, their mission being to persuade the British to halt their march on Lhasa. But the British invaders ignored the Tibetan local

The 13th Dalai Lama.

government's appeal for peace. With a few followers, the 13th Dalai Lama fled from Lhasa to Outer Mongolia. On August 3, 1904, the British occupied Lhasa. After the Dalai Lama had left Lhasa, the Qing court ordered that he be stripped of his titles temporarily.

In September 1904, the Qing central government refused to sign the British-dictated Lhasa Convention. The Qing government declared to the British that all items in the treaty should be drawn up by the Qing and British governments together, otherwise the Qing government would not take them into consideration. The Qing court decided that the war indemnity that the Tibetan local government had agreed to pay would be paid by the Qing central government.

At the end of 1904, the new cabinet of the British government, which badly needed to win Russia's support in the struggle against Germany, had to negotiate with the Qing on revisions to the Treaty of Lhasa. In January 1905, the Qing court and the British government held talks in Calcutta, India. During the talks, the British side demanded that the word "suzerainty" be used, in an attempt to write off China's sovereignty over Tibet. The negotiations became deadlocked.

The negotiations resumed in Beijing in 1906. The result was the Convention Between Great Britain and China Respecting Tibet, which included the Lhasa Convention as an annex. Article two of the 1906 convention stipulated: "The Government of Great Britain engages not to annex Tibetan territory or to interfere in the administration of Tibet. The Government of China also undertakes not to permit any other foreign state to interfere with the territory or internal administration of Tibet." Thus, the British government in effect recognized China's sovereignty over Tibet.

Chinese officials and the general population were not satisfied with the Qing's policy of compromise on the two British invasions of Tibet and they denounced the government. To consolidate its rule of Tibet and safeguard the southwestern border, the Qing government appointed Zhang Yintang as Tibet's assistant *amban* in April 1906. Of the hundreds of *ambans*, he was the only one of Han origin. In Lhasa, Zhang Yintang worked hard to implement his new administrative policy for Tibet, abolishing harmful practices, enforcing the rule of law, punishing corrupt officials, implementing political and economic reforms, and training troops. Some of his reform measures were divorced from Tibet's reality and some had their negative aspects. Because of the Qing government's corruption and the opposition of Tibetan conservatives, most of his measures were not put into practice. Nevertheless, his reforms aroused the hopes of Tibetan people and won their support. Zhang Yintang's administration of Tibet eventually aroused the suspicion and jealousy of the newly appointed *amban* Lian Yu. At the same time, the Qing court thought that the things he said and did were too radical and incompatible with the times. Consequently, Zhang Yintang was transferred to another post in May 1907.

At the instigation of the Siberian Buriyat Mongol monk Dorjieff, the 13th Dalai Lama fled from Lhasa to Outer Mongolia with the hope of winning Russia's support. At that time, Russia had just been defeated by Japan and was unable to give him material support, so the Dalai Lama still put his hopes in the Qing court. In response to a Qing request, he left Urga for Tibet in 1906. In November 1907, the Qing court approved his request for an interview with the emperor in Beijing. In January 1908, the Dalai Lama went to Mount Wutai before going to Beijing. Diplomatic envoys from Russia, the United States, Japan and Germany visited him on Mount Wutai. The British high commissioner to China made indirect contact with the

The Chensel Potrang, built in the Norbulingka for the 13th Dalai Lama.

Dalai Lama. At the end of September, the Dalai Lama left Mount Wutai for Beijing. Empress Dowager Cixi and Emperor Guangxu received the Dalai Lama several times in Beijing. The Qing government restored his Dalai Lama title and conferred on him the additional title, inscribed in a gold-leaf album, of the Loyally Submissive Vice-Regent, Great, Good, Self-Existent Buddha of Heaven.

However, the Dalai Lama was quite dissatisfied with the Qing court because the Qing government rejected his request to communicate directly with the emperor instead of through the *ambans*. The British high commissioner to China visited the Dalai Lama during his stay in Beijing. Meanwhile, the British government was working in every possible way to win the Dalai Lama over to its side. It was for this purpose that Captain Roderick O'Connor, Britain's Gyangzê-based commissioner in charge of commerce, was sent with a Drenjong prince to visit the Dalai Lama in Beijing. Consequently, after returning to Tibet, the Dalai Lama adopted a friendly attitude toward the British. He left Beijing for Tibet at the end of 1908 and arrived in Lhasa in November 1909.

The Qing reform of the *tusi* system (of appointing national-minority hereditary chieftains) and its dispatch of troops from Sichuan to Tibet threatened the political and economic interests of the upper strata of Tibet's clerical and secular circles. This caused conflict between the Qing government and part of Tibet's upper strata, headed by the Dalai Lama. To maintain his political power and interests, the 13th Dalai Lama changed his stand from one of resisting the British to one of relying on them.

The history of Tibet in this period, like that of the rest of China, saw its closed door to the outside world opened by force and the tranquility and calmness of several millennia broken.

Nenying Monastery (Kangmar County)

Nenying Monastery is in Nenying township, with Gyangzê County 10 kilometers to the north and Kangmar County 40 kilometers to the south. It

The rebuilt Nenying Monastery.

was built during the Tubo period by Padmasambhava's disciple Jampal Zangpo. It was expanded in successive generations. Originally the monastery contained a chapel, a pagoda, six *dratsangs* (colleges) and enclosing walls. It was initially a monastery of the Nyingma sect but later converted to the Kadam sect. In the 15th century, Tsongkhapa lived in the monastery for a time and constructed some buildings there. The monastery later converted to the Gelugpa sect. In the 19th century, the monastery was again expanded.

In an attempt to protect Gyangzê, Tibetan troops and Nenying Monastery monks used the monastery as a fortified base and waged a tough battle with the British invaders in 1904. The monastery was almost razed to the ground. Traces of the gunfire can still be seen. After the battle, the 13th Dalai Lama built an assembly hall east of the original Tubo chapel. The hall is now the monastery's equivalent of Lhasa's Jokhang Temple and is the main building of the present-day Nenying.

The most precious of the remaining cultural relics is a silk picture with Chinese characters that say: "Picture of Buddha made by order of the great Ming emperor on the 14th day of the fourth lunar month of the 10th year of the great Ming Yongle reign period." Next to the picture is a red ceramic cup inscribed with Chinese characters saying "Made in the great Ming Chenghua reign period" and a wood engraving of Buddhist stories.

As such an old monastery, Nenying has witnessed the wounds suffered by Tibet in the past and it holds a special place in history. Its value goes beyond that of a monastery.

On October 10, 1911, the Qing Dynasty was overthrown and the Republic of China was founded. The monarchical system, which had been in place for more than 2,000 years in China, finally came to an end. On January 1, 1912 in Nanjing, Dr. Sun Yat-sen became president of China's provisional government. He announced in his inaugural speech: "The foundation of the country lies in the people, and the unification of lands inhabited by the Han, Manchu, Mongol, Hui and Tibetan people into one country means the unification of the Han, Manchu, Mongol, Hui and Tibetan races. It is called national unification." The provisional constitution of the Republic of China, which was formulated under Sun Yat-sen's direction and proclaimed in March 1912, clearly stated that Tibet was part of the Republic of China's territory. In addition, the Law on the Organization of the Republic's Parliament stipulated a quota of five Tibetan deputies to be elected, Tibet being regarded as equal to the other provinces.

In April 1912, Yuan Shikai became president. He stated in a decree:

"Since all the areas inhabited by the Mongols, Tibetans, Huis and Uygurs are Chinese territory, the Mongols, Tibetans, Huis and Uygurs are citizens of China." The central government in Beijing established the Bureau of Mongolian and Tibetan Affairs. From then on, the constitution of the Republic of China always stated that Tibet was part of China. In October the same year, the 13th Dalai Lama wrote a letter from India to Kunzang Norbu, head of the Bureau of Mongolian and Tibetan Affairs, saying: "I hope Buddhism will be maintained. Please hand this letter to the central government for consideration." After receiving the letter, Yuan Shikai decreed the restoration of the Dalai Lama title and that of Loyally Submissive Vice-Regent, Great, Good, Self-Existent Buddha of Heaven. Yuan intended to send people to India to grant these titles to the 13th Dalai Lama but was unsuccessful because of obstruction by British India. In the middle of December 1912, the 13th Dalai Lama returned to Tibet.

A tripartite conference involving China, Britain and Tibet opened in Simla in India on October 13, 1913. At the outset of the conference, the British representative Henry McMahon instigated the Tibetan representative Lochen Shatra to raise the demands that Tibet become independent; that the boundary of Tibet should start south of Anding Tower and the Kunlun Mountains in southern Xinjiang, extend to the whole of Qinghai and encompass the western sections of Gansu and Sichuan, the regions around Tachienlu and those around Adunzi in northwestern Yunnan; and that no Chinese officials and troops be stationed in Tibet, and so on. It is worth noting that, behind the backs of the Chinese representatives, the British representative McMahon drew on a map a border between Tibet and British India that incorporated 90,000 square kilometers of Chinese territory into British India. Lochen Shatra did not dare report this to the Dalai Lama. Neither the Chinese central government nor the Tibetan local government approved this border. The British representative later presented a draft treaty that said Tibet would be divided into two zones, "Outer Tibet" and "Inner Tibet": Outer Tibet would include Lhasa, Shigatse and Qamdo, and Inner Tibet would include the rest of Tibet. China would have certain sovereignty over Inner Tibet but Outer Tibet would be autonomous. The Chinese government refused to sign the treaty. The First World War broke out in July 1914. Britain was unable to pay attention to the east, so the Simla conference came to nothing.

The British government later instigated a military invasion of Xikang (an area covering parts of present-day Tibet and Sichuan) by the Tibetan army. Although Tibetan troops pushed the border several hundred kilometers east, the war brought the Tibetan people a heavy burden. The Kashag had to reform the tax system. The increased taxation strained relations between the Kashag and the monasteries, and made the already bad relations between the Kashag and Tashilhunpo Monastery even worse. In 1923, the Kashag was beginning to impose levies of money, grain, troops and taxes in the Panchen Lama's domain. When Tashilhunpo objected, antagonism developed between the two factions. The ninth Panchen Lama had to flee Tibet in 1923, going to Beijing via Qinghai and Gansu.

In 1919, the Beijing government cabled the governor of Gansu, asking him to send Zhu Xiu and other people from Gansu to Tibet as special envoys to make friendly contact with the 13th Dalai Lama. The Dalai Lama told the envoys that he would not have turned to Britain had it not been for the high-handed treatment he had received from the *ambans*. He thanked the envoys for coming to Tibet and said he hoped that the president would soon appoint a plenipotentiary to settle the outstanding issues concerning Tibet. He assured Zhu Xiu that he was all in favor of the motherland and would work for the well-being of the five major ethnic groups. As for the draft treaty of Simla, the Dalai said it could be revised.

The Kuomintang (Nationalist Party) set up a national government in

Nanjing in 1929, and the ninth Panchen Lama set up an office in the city. The 13th Dalai Lama expressed the hope of restoring friendly relations with the central government. The Dalai Lama's Nanjing office was established in 1931 and acted as an official channel through which Tibet made contact with the central government. In the same year, the Kuomintang government convened a national conference in Nanjing and asked Tibet to send delegates. There were disputes between the Dalai Lama and Panchen Lama factions on the number of delegates. The Commission of Mongolian and Tibetan Affairs mediated between them. The Dalai Lama group eventually sent six voting delegates and three nonvoting delegates, while the Panchen Lama group sent four voting delegates and five nonvoting delegates. The ninth Panchen Lama arrived in Nanjing and attended the meeting at the invitation of the Nationalist government. He also gave a lecture entitled "Tibet is Part of Chinese Territory" to the third session of the New Asia Society in Nanjing. His lecture used historical facts to confirm that Tibet was part of China. He expressed his desire for the early restoration of Tibet's previous subordinate status to the Chinese central government. He called for all of China's ethnic groups to unite and resist the foreign invasion. In July 1931, the Nationalist government officially conferred on the ninth Panchen Lama the title of Great Master of Infinite Wisdom, Defender of the Nation and Propagator of the Doctrine, together with a jade seal and a certificate recording the title. In December 1932, the Nationalist government asked the Panchen Lama to visit Nanjing again so they could all discuss matters concerning Tibet and his return home. At the same time, the Nationalist government officially announced the Panchen Lama's appointment as the Western Border Area Publicity Commissioner.

In April 1933, the Panchen Lama sent Ngachen Rinpoche and other high-ranking lamas to Lhasa to meet the Dalai Lama. The Dalai Lama expressed his desire for the Panchen Lama's early return. He promised to return the Panchen Lama's former domains to him upon his return. However, the promise remained unfulfilled. The 13th Dalai Lama died in Lhasa in 1933, on the 30th day of the 10th month of the Tibetan lunar calendar. In December 1933, the Kuomintang government granted the Dalai Lama the posthumous title of Great Master of Patriotism, Magnanimity, Benevolence and Sagacity. The government held a big memorial meeting for him in Nanjing.

Shortly after the 13th Dalai Lama died, changes took place in Tibet's ruling clique. Some events dealt a heavy blow to the pro-British separatist forces in Tibet.

More and more Tibetan clergy and lay people expressed their hope that the Panchen Lama would return. In March 1935, the Panchen Lama presented the Nationalist government with his plan to return to Tibet via Qinghai. He said he hoped that the Nationalist government would send a high-ranking official to escort him back to Tibet and offer advice as to how the Panchen Lama could spread Buddhism and oversee the development of Tibet. He also said he hoped that the Nationalist government would allocate special funds for his work. His plan was approved in June. The problem of an armed escort accompanying the Panchen Lama on his way back to Tibet was not solved because the Kashag did not permit the Panchen Lama to take a single Han official or soldier to Tibet. The Panchen Lama's hope of returning to Tibet could not come true. He became ill from anxiety and grief and died on December 1, 1937 in Yushu, Qinghai Province.

After the 13th Dalai Lama died, the Reting Hutuktu Jampel Yeshe Tenzin Gyaltsen (1910-47) was appointed regent. The search began for the reincarnation of the 13th Dalai Lama.

The 14th Dalai Lama was enthroned at the Potala on February 22, 1940.

The 14th Dalai Lama's enthronement ceremony.

The enthronement ceremony was attended by 500 people, including the regent, the Silon, the *kalons*, other Kashag officials, grand incarnate lamas, representatives of the three great monasteries, the central government representative Wu Zhongxin and his entourage, and representatives of Nepal and Bhutan in Lhasa. The British-Indian representatives did not take part in the day's ceremonial activities. On March 8, the Tibetan local government sent a cable to the central government to express its thanks for sending a special envoy to attend the enthronement ceremony.

Before leaving Lhasa in April 1940, Wu Zhongxin secured the Kashag's consent to set up a Tibet office of the Nationalist government's Commission of Mongolian and Tibetan Affairs.

After the Dalai Lama ascended the throne, the regent Reting Hutuktu's prestige increased day after day. During Reting's regency, relations improved between Tibet and the central government. Unhappy about the regent's close ties with the central government, Britain and pro-British elements instigated a smear campaign by some monks and lay officials in the Kashag, with the aim of forcing him out of office. They spread rumors falsely accusing the regent of having intimate relations with some women. The rumors quite upset the young regent Reting. The pro-British elements made the Nechung Chosgyong prophesy a three-year "misfortune" for Reting and advise him to leave office temporarily and meditate in confinement to ward off evil spirits. To defuse the attack, Reting requested and obtained from the Kashag a three-year leave of absence in January 1941 and turned his duties over to his tutor, the Taktra Rinpoche. Reting picked

Taktra, who was 67 years old, because he thought that, with Taktra as acting regent, it would be easy for him, Reting, to resume the regency at the end of the three-year leave. Reting sent a cable to the central government, announcing his resignation from office and Taktra's succession as regent. When Reting left Lhasa for Reting Monastery, Taktra showed his gratitude by holding a grand farewell ceremony for him along with all the monks, lay officials and *khenpos* (learned abbots) of the three great monasteries, and Tibetan officers and soldiers.

After becoming regent, Taktra dismissed and replaced Reting's followers with pro-British elements. Consequently, Taktra took control of the Kashag, and Tibet's relations with the central government worsened rapidly. In a surprise move in the summer of 1943, instigated by Hugh E. Richardson, Britain's representative in Lhasa, the Kashag announced the establishment of a Foreign Affairs Bureau and notified the Lhasa office of the Commission of Mongolian and Tibetan Affairs that the office would

Reting Rinpoche.

henceforth have to deal with the bureau rather than the local government. The commission refused to have anything to do with the Foreign Affairs Bureau. The Kuomintang government also refused to recognize the bureau and it ordered troops in Sichuan and Qinghai to prepare to solve the problem with force. The Kashag was forced to set up another body to deal with the Commission of Mongolian and Tibetan Affairs. The government of British India gave the Kashag modern weapons and instigated Taktra to establish an English school that was to recruit the children of aristocrats. This aroused bitter resistance from the monks of the three great monasteries.

In April 1944, Chiang Kai-shek appointed Shen Zonglian, one of his attendants, as head of the Nationalist government's Lhasa office. The Nationalist government decided to increase its propaganda in Tibet and strengthen ties with the Panchen Lama group and those supporting the central government. After a three-year absence from office, Reting went to Lhasa under the pretext of attending the opening ceremony of the Je Dratsang Assembly Hall in Sera Monastery. He hoped to discuss with Taktra his resumption of the post of regent. When they met, Taktra, who had become powerful by that time, did not say a word about it. Reting had to return to his monastery in northern Tibet. After he resigned, Reting maintained close relations with the central government. When officials from the Commission of Mongolian and Tibetan Affairs went to visit him, he expressed the wish to reassume the post of regent with the central government's support and he offered his service to the government. In May 1945, the Reting Hutuktu and Losang Gyaltsen were elected alternate members of the Kuomintang central committee at its sixth plenary session. Taktra knew that Reting was still a strong opponent. To elevate his own position, Taktra granted himself the title of Gyalpo Hutuktu during a meeting of the Tsongdu (national assembly) in June 1946. This had never happened before.

The discord between Reting and Taktra became increasingly intense. On April 14, 1947, the Kashag sent 200 troops to arrest Reting at Reting Monastery. After Reting was taken to Lhasa, several hundred armed monks from Sera Monastery stormed into Lhasa in an unsuccessful attempt to rescue Reting from prison. The Kuomintang government contacted Taktra and the Kashag by telegraph after Reting's arrest in an effort to rescue him. The monks' resistance made Taktra more fearful of Reting's influence, so Taktra decided to get rid of Reting. On May 7, the Reting Hutuktu was murdered in prison.

After the "Reting incident," pro-British elements headed by Taktra intensified their activities. In October 1947, the Kashag organized a trade mission to visit the United States and Britain for a trade "survey." The aim was to win recognition of Tibet as an independent country by the British and US governments. The mission ran into a number of problems when it arrived in India. One of the problems was to do with passports and visas. These problems took the mission to Nanjing in early 1948. The Nationalist government tried to dissuade the mission from going on its trip and said that, if the members of the mission insisted on going, they must carry Chinese passports. Ignoring the warnings of the Nationalist government, the mission secretly contacted the US ambassador to China, John L. Stuart. Through Stuart, the mission obtained visas for the United States from the US consul general in Hong Kong, using the illegal "passports" issued by the Kashag. In Hong Kong, to get foreign currency, the mission sold Indian businessmen an export license for raw silk that the Nationalist government had issued to the Kashag. With this foreign currency, the mission bought air tickets and flew to the United States. From the United States, they went to Britain, France, Switzerland, Italy and India. But none of these countries would recognize Tibet as an independent country. The mission members eventually had to return to Lhasa.

The history of Tibet in the period of the Republic of China, short as it was, was as changeable as the international situation and very eventful. During that period, the channels between the local Tibetan government and the central government were unblocked, notwithstanding all the difficulties in their relationship. The central government administered Tibet effectively, while the broad masses of the Tibetan people had a sense of allegiance to

China. *Few monasteries were built during this period because Tibetan Buddhism had already developed to a certain stage.*

Chokhorgyal Monastery and Lhamoi Lhatso Lake (Gyaca County in Shannan Prefecture)

Chokhorgyal Monastery was founded in 1509 by the second Dalai Lama, Gendun Gyatso. When Gendun Gyatso came to Dakpo to propagate the doctrines of the Gelugpa sect, he was fascinated by the charming Lhamoi Lhatso (Oracle Lake) and so built a monastery by it. In 1512, the lamas of Tashilhunpo Monastery asked Gendun Gyatso to be their monastery's abbot because he had contributed greatly to the Gelugpa sect. As Tashilhunpo abbot, Gendun Gyatso had the monastery expanded. Then he took on the position of abbot at Drepung and Sera monasteries and he became head of the Gelugpa sect. From then on, he lived in Drepung Monastery during spring and winter, and spent summer and autumn in Chokhorgyal. It was then that Chokhorgyal and Lhamoi Lhatso began to be considered sacred sites of the Gelugpa sect. The reflections on Lhamoi Lhatso, the Oracle Lake, were said to indicate future events. During searches for the reincarnation of the Dalai Lama, Panchen Lama and other high-ranking incarnate lamas, the local Tibetan government would send a high-ranking lama to the lake to pray and look at its reflections, using these to decide where the reincarnation would be. This was a required procedure in the search for an incarnate lama's reincarnation. Following the death of the 13th Dalai Lama, Regent Reting went to Chokhorgyal Monastery to look at the lake's reflections, and said that the reincarnation of the 13th Dalai Lama had been born in the east. So the Kashag organized three search parties and sent them to southeastern Tibet, Kham and Qinghai in the autumn of 1936. The party headed by Kalzang Rinpoche discovered the boy reincarnation called Lhamo Thondup, who later became the 14th Dalai Lama, in Qijiachuan

(Taktser in Tibetan) in Ping'an County, Qinghai Province. All the Dalai Lamas would go to Chokhorgyal to worship the goddess Palden Lhamo, who was said to be the Dalai Lama's protector. Many tourists and pilgrims now visit the monastery and lake.

Shide Ling Temple (Reting Labrang, Lhasa)

Shide Ling Temple, southwest of Ramoche Temple in Lhasa, was the residential seat in Lhasa of the Reting Hutuktu. The Reting Hutuktu was an influential figure in Tibetan history. He was one of the incarnate lamas who had been regent in the local Tibetan government.

The small temple was founded at the time of the Tubo *tsanpo* Tri Ralpachen but it was damaged in the ninth century when Lang Darma was persecuting Buddhism. It was rebuilt and expanded during the Yuan Dynasty.

Shide Ling's main buildings include an assembly hall, chapels, and monks' living quarters. In the center of the temple is a square courtyard. At the back of the courtyard are the assembly hall and chapels. On the other three sides are the monks' quarters and the kitchen. The assembly hall is nine rooms wide and sevens room long. It has 48 columns and colorfully painted walls. Behind the assembly hall are three chapels and there are corridors in front of the hall doors. There are small rooms on either side.

Shide Ling was expanded on a large scale during the Qing Dynasty but it was badly destroyed in 1862 and razed to the ground in 1947 at the time of the "Reting incident."

There used to be a hundred residential rooms in several two-story flat-roofed buildings but most of these have been destroyed. However, what remains of the temple buildings still gives an indication of its original style and features.

With the victory of the Chinese revolution under the leadership of the Chinese Communist Party, Tibetan history entered a new phase. In 1951, the Dalai Lama sent a delegation of the local Tibetan government headed by Ngabo Ngawang Jigme to Beijing to negotiate the peaceful liberation of Tibet with a delegation of the central government headed by Li Weihan. It took the negotiators just one month to reach an agreement. On May 23, 1951, the Agreement of the Central People's Government and the Local Government of Tibet on Measures for the Peaceful Liberation of Tibet (called the 17-Point Agreement for short) was signed. The peace agreement not only clearly defined the relationship between Tibet and the central government but also ended the disharmony between the Dalai Lama and Panchen Lama. The agreement also put an end to Tibet's semicolonial period. Tibet then entered a new epoch. Under the leadership of the Chinese Communist Party, Tibet has achieved a great deal socially, economically and culturally. The Tibetan people are now leading prosperous and happy lives.

Appendixes

1. Folklore and Festivals in Tibet

(1) Marriage and the Family in Tibet

Marriages in Tibet have traditionally been mostly monogamous. If a poor family had several sons, only one son would remain at home and he would get married and inherit the family property. The other sons would be sent to monasteries and become monks or, when they grew up, marry into other families. Monogamous marriages were more popular in pastoral areas than in agricultural areas because herdsmen led itinerant lives and a tent was too small to accommodate a lot of people.

There was a type of monogamous marriage

A Tibetan child.

called "kiss marriage" (*khathug* in Tibetan). This type of marriage was practiced among poor peasants and herdsmen. The so-called kiss marriage was when a young man and woman who loved each other left their parents and lived as husband and wife without going through any wedding ceremony. Their parents, too poor to arrange any wedding ceremony for them, preferred to give them some furniture and cattle so the young couple could live independently. This was how this simple form of marriage emerged.

Generally, Tibetan men and women married the partners of their choice. It was uncommon for marriages to be arranged solely by the parents. Arranged marriages were usually practiced in rich families, who focused on matching social status and wealth. In some areas, cousins on the mother's side were allowed to marry. In other areas, this type of marriage was prohibited because of the close blood relationship. As for the requirements for a bride and groom, a man was required to be able to read and write, while a woman had to be able to do business, know how to use coins, and be good at doing housework.

Tibetan weddings differ from place to place but generally go through the following stages:

Engagement: After the decision has been made for them to get married, the future bride and groom go to a monastery to exchange vows and betrothal objects, such as bootlaces, belts, bracelets and swords.

Marriage offer: Whether or not the parents had arranged the marriage, the future groom goes to the future bride's family to make an offer of marriage. The procedure is carried out by a go-between and the young man himself. Both sides discuss the number of betrothal gifts and when to give them, the time of the wedding, and the number of guests.

Wedding ceremony: The day before the wedding, the bride's family has a party, with the guests drinking and dancing until evening. At sunset, the bride sings the "Combing the Hair Song."

The bridal group usually consists of eight people, although the number is not fixed. The future bride's brother leads her horse. On the way, the future groom's family offers ceremonial toasts to the bridal party, sings drinking songs and says auspicious words.

When the group members arrive at the groom's house, they are greeted with a wedding feast. The guests sit on the right side and the hosts on the left and they all drink liquor and sing songs. Then the guest and host in the respective top seats hold a bowl of milk and a cup of liquor, and sprinkle out the milk and liquor three times with a pine twig dipped in the cup. They exchange greetings and drink tea. Then the wedding feast begins. The best part is considered to be when the drinking songs are sung. Wedding celebrations usually last for three days. During this time, friends and relatives visit to present *katag* ceremonial scarves and wedding gifts. In turn, they are entertained with barley beer and butter tea and there is singing and dancing.

A wedding ceremony includes the following stages:

"The showing of the clothes": The bridegroom's gifts and the bride's dowry are displayed.

Changchen ("big liquor"): As songs are sung continually until midnight, several people carry a big liquor jar into the room, pretending that the jar is very heavy. At this moment, someone says some words of praise, giving the banquet a happy atmosphere.

Tsong: The *tsong* ritual is held the following morning after breakfast. A sheep is dismembered and distributed among those entitled, who say auspicious words.

Sosa ("shoulder blade"): When the bridal group accompanies the bride to the groom's family and praises the groom, the bride offers each member of the group a cup of tea. Meanwhile, someone praises the history and role of the shoulder blade. The rite might have developed from ancient divination practices.

Gashitsa (words of blessing): This ritual is held at noon. The bride and groom sit on a white carpet and hold in their hands a dish of highland barley and a cup of liquor. Young guests sprinkle water on the couple's heads and necks and then the dish is given to an elderly man, who utters words of blessing.

At the end of the ceremony, people sing the song "Trashi" (meaning "auspicious conclusion"). When the bridal party bids farewell to the host, the host again offers a toast. After the guests mount their horses, they go away and turn back three times before taking their leave at last. Sometimes the bride also goes with them back to her parents' home.

After the wedding celebration, the bride lives in her parents' home for three months and then goes to her husband's home. Her parents give her gifts at this time. Her father and a good friend accompany her to her husband's home and return after staying there for seven days. The groom's parents give the guests cheese and pastries as gifts on their departure.

At the proper time, the bride's parents invite their son-in-law to their home. When he says good-bye to them, they give him a horse as a present. This marks the end of the whole wedding ceremony.

The Tibetan family unit is basically the nuclear family. Most households consist of only two generations – parents and children. Households of three generations are rare and those of four generations extremely rare.

The family is important to Tibetans. To keep intact, a large family always chooses one of the children, a son or daughter, as a successor who is allowed to stay in the home after getting married. The others have to be married off or become monks or nuns. Some sons and daughters remain unmarried throughout their lives. The unmarried regard their nieces and nephews as their own children.

Tibetans often intermarry with people of other ethnic groups. These mixed families also lead harmonious, happy lives.

(2) Funeral Rites in Tibet

For historical and religious reasons and because of outside influences, several different kinds of funerals are practiced in Tibet: interment, water funerals, sky burials or celestial burials, cremation and stupa burials, as well as tree, wall and house burials. Attitudes to them differ in different areas because Tibet is large and areas differ in their cultural development.

Generally speaking, when a man dies, his immediate family informs the other relatives of his death, and relatives and friends go to offer condolences. A local lama prays day and night for the release of the soul of the deceased.

For 49 days after the death, monks chant sutras for the deceased in his house, where butter lamps burn on an altar. The corpse is kept in the deceased's home for between three and seven days. At the end of the funeral, a high-ranking lama gathers the whole village and chants the Lamaist six-syllable mantra "Om mani padme hum" or an eight-word magic mantra of the Bon religion. The deceased's family gives alms, such as candy or rice with meat, to gain merit on behalf of the deceased.

Celestial burials or sky burials: This form of burial was traditionally used for almost all those who died in Tibet, excluding those who died an unnatural death. It was practiced in almost all pastoral areas and in some agricultural areas. The ritual is carried out by monks or lay caretakers on a special site for celestial burials. The body is laid on the rocky platform, males face up and females face down. A pile of smoldering juniper leaves and incense made of *tsampa* (barley flour) form a huge cloud of smoke to inform the vultures of the occasion. The monks' prayers assist this process. The body is systematically cut up. After being sliced into pieces, the flesh is set aside and the bones are crushed, mixed with *tsampa* and rolled into a ball. The offering to the vultures commences with the ball of crushed bone, followed by the slices of flesh. If no vultures come or if they do not want to eat, this means that the deceased was a grave sinner, so his family has to ask the monks to pray for him until the vultures eat up his body. Outsiders are forbidden from watching the burial.

The celestial burial practiced by Tibetans as a form of funeral is directly connected with their nature worship and Buddhism. This kind of burial is based on the Buddhist concept of almsgiving, which is typically described in the story of King Shivi rescuing a dove: A dove being chased by an eagle hid in the armpit of King Shivi. The king asked the eagle why it was chasing the dove. The eagle answered that it did so because it was hungry. The king gave the eagle his own flesh in order to save the dove. Another moving story about almsgiving is that of Mahasattva feeding a tiger with his own body. The two stories express the sacred ideal of sacrificing oneself to save another's life. This concept is developed from that of mercy.

The celestial burial is also a way of giving alms and offering sacrifices. The manner of disposing of one's body is considered a final act of generosity that enables other animals to be nourished by one's remains. The burial has three levels of meaning: (1) Offering one's body to vultures is a way of saving them; (2) Offering the body as a sacrifice is a form of blood sacrifice as practiced in ancient times; and (3) The celestial burial is based on the Buddhist concept of *bardo* (the intermediate state between death and rebirth). When a death occurs, monks are invited to chant prayers from *The Tibetan Book of the Dead* ("bar-do-thos-gros" in Tibetan) in order to give the deceased's soul an earlier rebirth. The celestial burial seems to be faster and cleaner than interment and water burial.

Cremation: In ancient times, this form of burial was permitted for lamas and people of noble birth. It was later practiced among the general population.

Generally speaking, a Tibetan village will have one or two cremation sites. The day for holding a great lama's funeral is decided through divination by the lama himself before his death. A cremation platform is made of earth and grass, is a meter high, and has wind holes underneath. It is built a day or two before the funeral, which is held in the early morning. Two or four people carry the coffin with the deceased's body inside to the platform, on which piles of wood have been placed. When the coffin is placed on the platform to face west, butter is spread on the coffin and the body. Then they are set on fire as monks chant prayers. The burning-up of the coffin and body in a big fire is considered an auspicious omen.

After the cremation, the ashes are taken to high up in the mountains and scattered to the winds, thrown into a river or kept in an urn. The deceased person's family entertains those attending the funeral with feasts. Monks chant prayers day and night before the funeral but only during the daytime after the funeral. The family of a person who has died an unnatural death stresses the importance of chanting prayers to release his soul.

People believe that there will be rain the day after a cremation to wash up the evil it brought.

Interment: Old people are buried in locations at a high altitude while the young are buried lower down.

The body, wrapped in cloth, is placed in a coffin in a sitting or reclining position. Coffin for bodies in a sitting position are more popular than those for the reclining position. The body in a sitting position is tied up into a small bundle. The coffin for such a body is therefore smaller and can be carried easily by two people.

The coffin is buried in a pit dug into the ground at a place selected by a lama through divination. The tomb is in the form of a cone, with a prayer flag on top. At the end, those attending the funeral scatter sacrificial objects around the tomb. Once the burial is over, the coffin bearers or undertakers go to the deceased's home to wash themselves and are entertained with feasts.

Water burial: This form of burial is practiced by Tibetans living by rivers. This form of burial is usually used for children and poor people. The body is taken to the river and thrown into the torrent of water at a time selected through divination, having first been torn limb from limb as in celestial burials.

Stupa burial: This is a very distinguished form of burial reserved for great lamas only. Salt water is applied to the body, which is then dried and later smeared with precious ointments and perfumes, then embalmed in a stupa. The body sits with the legs crossed. In another form of burial, the ashes of a body that has been cremated may also be placed in a stupa. Kept in monastery halls, stupas vary greatly depending on the rank of the occupant. The materials used to make stupas include gold, silver, bronze, wood and earth. Dalai Lamas and Panchen Lamas are given gold stupas. The stupa for the fifth Dalai Lama is 14.85 meters high, covered in 110,000 *liang* (3,410 kilograms) of gold leaf and decorated with jewels. The brilliant and magnificent-looking stupa consists of a base, a body and a top. A common stupa is made of stone and clay, with four or six sides.

After a funeral, regardless of the form of burial, prayer flags of white, yellow and red cloth are tied on poles, each flag being between 20 and 35 centimeters wide and 3 meters long. They are put around the house and tomb of the deceased as sacrifices to release the soul of the dead. The monks who chant sutras for the deceased are paid according to how long they perform this service. To release the soul of the deceased, funeral gifts should be offered to great lamas. Gifts might include cattle or horses. On the deceased's anniversary, the family will invite monks to chants sutras.

(3) Costumes

The main feature of Tibetan clothing is that it envelops the wearer in huge, loose-fitting, long-sleeved garments, loosely tied at the waist. The styles and materials vary between agricultural and pastoral areas. There were different styles of traditional costume for men and women, for children, adults and old people, and for nobles and commoners. Monks and officials also have their own form of dress.

The Tibetan gown or *tuba* is the traditional Tibetan costume and is suitable

Tibetan robes.

for the weather conditions of the Tibetan plateau, where the temperature varies widely between morning and evening and between winter and summer. Simple, loose-fitting Tibetan garments are chiefly made from Tibetan tweed although some are made from serge, brocade, linen and cloth. The gowns have a wide left lapel, which is fastened under the right sleeve with either buttons or cloth ribbons. Men's gowns are usually made of black or white tweed edged with a narrow cotton or silk border in a contrasting color around the collar, sleeves, lapel and hem. Those of women are made of red, black, blue or green tweed. Splendidly rich dresses are made of serge, tweed and brocade edged with tiger, leopard or otter fur, and wide strips of velvet or woven wool.

In pastoral areas, the gowns are made of sheepskin covered with black and brown brocade, edged along the collar and hem with strips of otter fur and brocade. In agricultural areas, the gowns are made of cloth.

A shirt is worn under the outer garment. Before the garment is tied with a sash around the waist, the front of the garment is raised well above the knee for men and above the shoes for women. This creates a huge pouch, which is used to store all kinds of useful articles. In summer, the right arm is slipped out, and the right sleeve is slung over the right shoulder. In winter, both arms are kept warm in the sleeves. A silk or velvet sash is indispensable when wearing the gown. The front of the tied garment is flat and the back is folded.

Tibetan gowns are large and loose fitting. These all-purpose garments may be used as blankets when sleeping, while the arms can be slipped out and the sleeves tied round the waist on warm days.

Hats: Tibetans have a wide variety of hats for both men and women, which differ in style from region to region. Brocade fur hats and wide-brimmed felt hats are very popular among Tibetans. They wear fur hats in winter. Felt hats are popular in pastoral areas, young people wearing black ones, and old and middle-aged people wearing white ones. The hats are shaped like a cone or cylinder.

Hats being made.

Boots: Tibetans traditionally wear boots. The boots' legs are made of felt, tweed and black or red tanned yak skin. A 10 or 15-centimeter slit at the back makes the boots easy to put on and take off. The boots are characterized by upturned toes. A boot's leg is joined to its lower part by beautiful strips of colored brocade and woolen cloth.

Tibetan adornments: Tibetans love to wear adornments. Both men and women alike love them, especially in pastoral regions. Men wear a piece of flint, a purse or a small dagger tied to the waist as adornments. The dagger's sheath is made of silver or is gilded, its handle decorated with pieces of agate. A wide range of adornments can be found, such as rings, bracelets, earrings, necklaces, snuff boxes, amulets of gold and silver, together with finely crafted daggers, pouches and flint. Amulets or charm boxes, which contain mantras or the image of a deity, have long been used by Tibetans to ward off evil spirits and to clear away obstacles in the wearer's life. Gold, silver, ivory, coral and jade are the most popular materials for fashioning jewelry, which can be worn on the head, neck, chest, waist, back, arms and fingers.

Tibetans, especially the women, are very particular about how they wear their hair. In pastoral areas, men wear their hair in one strand, plaited with red, black and blue cords and wound around their head. Women wear their hair in one or two strands, studded with coral and agate and either wound around their heads or hanging behind. The lower part of the strands is enveloped in a cover decorated with silver and amber. With women, the number of plaits indicates their marital status – unmarried women wear a single plait or one thick plait with many small ones, while married women wear two plaits or two thick plaits with many small ones. Some widows shave their heads to indicate that they will not marry again. If no colorful cords are worn in the plaits, this indicates that the person has suffered a bereavement.

Aprons, or *pangdan*, are popular adornments typical of Tibetan women. The aprons have stripes of red, yellow, blue, green and white. The best-quality aprons are known as *shadma* and are neatly woven in between 14 and 20 different colors. More commonly found are the *putag* aprons, which are of lower quality.

One of the most famous places for the weaving of aprons in Tibet is Chideshol District, Gongkar County, Shannan Prefecture. Aprons have been woven in this village – known as the "apron village" – for five or six centuries and its products are highly prized.

The costumes and ornaments of Tibetan women.

Monks' clothes: Monks wear a *kashaya*, a patchwork outer vestment of purple-red felt. They wrap their bodies in long pieces of cloth and wear robes, tall boots and special monks' hats.

(4) Tibetan Food and Drink

Traditional Food and Drink

Tsampa, or barley flour, is the staple food of Tibetans, particularly in pastoral areas. It is convenient to store and carry and also to eat when away from home, as *tsampa* packed into a leather pouch provides a meal in itself.

Highly nutritious, *tsampa* is made from sun-dried barley that has been roasted and ground into flour. There are also varieties of *tsampa* made from peas, corn and oats, as well as dried beef in pastoral areas.

Tsampa is eaten by adding a little of the flour to some butter tea in a bowl, kneading the mixture into a dough with the fingers and then breaking

Locals from the Tsang area.

off a tiny portion, rolling it into a ball and eating it. Another way to serve *tsampa* involves cooking a kind of *tsampa* broth, which is a mixture of barley flour with plain tea, butter tea or milk tea. The broth is always served to children and sick people. The third way, known as *kati*, involves putting *tsampa* into a bowl, pressing it with the fingers, pouring plain tea, butter tea or milk tea into the bowl, drinking the tea and then eating the *tsampa*.

In addition to *tsampa*, buckwheat, corn powder and wheat are Tibetans' other staple foods.

Tibetans eat beef, mutton and pork. Beef and mutton are staple foods in pastoral areas. They use knives instead of chopsticks to eat meat. The meat can be prepared in three ways – as a meat *tsampa*, boiled meat, or dried raw meat. The meat is cut into big chunks before being boiled. Meat that is to be dried is also cut into chunks and then hung up when the temperature drops below freezing point. When the dried meat is ready, it is taken down to be roasted or eaten as it is.

Vegetables eaten in Tibetan areas include radishes, taros, cabbages, turnips, hot peppers, onions, and garlic. Taro is a favorite vegetable of Tibetans. In winter, Tibetans make pickled radish leaves, which can be stored away conveniently. The pickled leaves may be fried or made into a soup. Tibet has a variety of fungi, which are highly nutritious and good for entertaining friends.

Dairy products are an indispensable part of the Tibetan diet. Milk is either drunk directly or used to make dairy products such as milk tea, butter, yogurt, curd and cheese.

Butter is a basic necessity for Tibetans. It is highly nutritious, which is important for Tibetans, especially those in pastoral areas. Butter is used in a number of ways, mainly to make butter tea but it is also eaten mixed with *tsampa* and used to deep-fry doughnuts – that is, flour, butter, sugar and water mixed into a paste and then cooked in a deep layer of fat.

Tea is an indispensable part of Tibetan life and is always served to guests.

There is plain tea, *tsampa* tea, milk tea, butter tea, sweetened tea, roasted-flour tea, and so on.

Plain tea is very easy to prepare. It is made simply by adding salt to boiled tea. Tibetans usually drink it in the afternoon. This tea is also used to mix with *tsampa*.

Tsampa tea is prepared by putting a little *tsampa* into a bowl, pressing the *tsampa* with the fingers to prevent it from floating up when water is added, and finally adding butter, milk residue, sugar and then plain tea.

Milk tea can quench the thirst, promote digestion and relieve fatigue. It is an everyday drink in pastoral and semipastoral areas. Milk tea is made by putting brick tea into water, boiling the tea and water until it is coffee-colored, and then adding milk.

Butter tea is highly nutritious. It is an everyday drink among Tibetans and is served to visitors. Butter tea is made by removing the tea leaves from freshly brewed brick tea, then putting the tea into a "tea churn" along with milk, fresh eggs, butter, salt and some boiling water. This combination is then churned for a minute or so until the tea is well mixed. The resulting liquid is poured into a kettle and then served. Walnuts, peanuts and sesame seeds are sometimes added to the tea. Since butter is the main ingredient, butter tea is a very warming drink and a good antidote to the cold, so it is especially suited to high altitudes.

Before work, a Tibetan will drink several bowlfuls of butter tea. The Tibetan custom is to drink butter tea in separate sips, with the host refilling the bowl to the brim after each sip. In this way, the guest never drains his bowl because it is constantly topped up. If the visitor does not wish to drink, the best thing to do is leave the tea untouched until the time comes to leave and then drain the bowl. Etiquette is thus observed and the host will not be offended.

Sweetened tea is made by putting milk and sugar into freshly brewed black tea and mixing them. The resulting liquid is sweetened tea, which has a very good flavor. It is a favorite drink of Tibetans in Ü-Tsang (Lhasa,

Shannan and Shigatse). The tea is very easy to prepare and contains less fat, so more and more young people like to drink it.

Roasted-flour tea is prepared by putting roasted *tsampa* flour into boiling water and, after mixing, adding powdered tea and salt. The resulting liquid is flour tea.

Tibetans all enjoy barley beer, a traditional drink in Tibetan areas. With an alcohol content of 15 to 20%, barley beer is slightly milky with a somewhat sweet tangy taste.

Tibetan utensils for food and drink

The utensils used for food and drink in Tibetan areas are distinctive. Every Tibetan household has a churn for butter tea and a pot for milk tea. Utensils are made of copper in Tibetan-inhabited areas of Yunnan, while they are wooden and painted red, brown or yellow in other Tibetan areas. High-quality utensils are silver-coated. In pastoral areas, it is quite common to see Tibetans carrying knives, daggers or swords at their waist. Nomads use knives to slaughter and skin livestock and to cut up wood to make a tent. The making of daggers and knives in Tibetan areas has a long history and also involves exquisite skills.

A butter-tea churn is an absolute necessity in a Tibetan household as it is used day in and day out. Two types of churns are used in Tibet. The larger kind is commonly found in pastoral areas, where it is used to churn butter. The smaller kind is used for making yak-butter tea. The smaller churns are often carried on journeys.

Small wooden bowls are always carried wherever Tibetans go, tucked into the front of their gown. A bowl is thus always at hand for drinking tea or kneading *tsampa* while up in the mountains cutting firewood or when out in the fields. Nobody thinks it at all impolite when a visitor reaches into his gown and brings out his wooden bowl for the host to fill with tea or a handful of *tsampa*.

Tibetan bellows have their own unique style. They comprise a sheepskin bag connected to an iron pipe. One hand or both are used to work the bellows, pressing the sheepskin bag and thus forcing the air through the iron pipe into a charcoal or yak-dung fire. These bellows are durable and easy to use and common all over Tibet.

The main fuel is wood in agricultural areas, while it is dried yak dung in pastoral areas.

(5) Other Tibetan Customs

The offering of *katag* **scarves:** A *katag* is a ceremonial scarf made of silk or hemp cloth. Presenting a *katag* is the most usual form of courtesy. *Katags* are offered at weddings, funerals, festivals, audiences with elders, during a pilgrimage, when sending or receiving greetings, seeing people

A *katag* scarf being offered.

off on long journeys, and so on. The offering of the *katag* expresses blessings, celebration, respect, friendship, condolences and sympathy. The way in which the scarf is offered varies according to the occasion. When a *katag* is offered to an elder, the giver will present it with both hands upward, putting it on the table or through somebody else. When the scarf is given to a man of a younger generation, the scarf is put around his neck. When the recipient is of the same generation, it is presented to him directly.

The most common color of *katag* is white. Since ancient times, Tibetans have considered white a symbol of purity, so *katags* are usually this color. *Katags* may also be multicolored in green, white, yellow, blue and red. Blue symbolizes the sky, white signifies the clouds, green symbolizes water, yellow stands for the earth, and red for fire. The five-colored scarf is the highest courtesy and reserved only for special occasions.

The offering of sacrificial objects: Tibetans often offer sacrificial objects to images of Buddhas and Bodhisattvas to express their worship. Tibetan families usually offer pure water to Buddha images in the morning and light butter lamps on the altar in the evening. During festivals, every family will lay offerings to Buddha images in the shrine at home and also go to monasteries to present offerings, light butter lamps before the images and give alms to monks.

Prostration: Prostrating oneself is a traditional form of courtesy. People usually prostrate themselves before Buddhist images, stupas and incarnate lamas.

There are two ways to prostrate oneself. Ordinary prostration is performed before Buddhist images at home. Another kind of special prostration, known as full prostration, is performed on pilgrimage to monasteries. Full prostration needs devotion and courage. There are always crowds of people fully prostrating themselves in a clockwise direction around monasteries and other famous places. In a full prostration, the whole body lies flat on the ground with the arms stretching straight out in front. The following prostration begins from where the hands last touched the ground. Full prostration is very hard, so those doing it always wear gloves and kneepads. Perpetual prostration over the ages has left deep traces on the ground or floorboards in front of monastery or chapel gates.

Turning prayer wheels: In Tibetan-inhabited areas, there are always Tibetans, especially old people, holding and turning a *manichorkor* or prayer

Prostration: the act of lying face down to show submission.

wheel. It is believed that one turn of a prayer wheel is equivalent to reading a sutra several times. There are also big prayer wheels lined up along the walls of shrines and monasteries. Some villages have built houses especially for prayer wheels. Prayer wheels vary in size, form and quality. They are filled with rolls of paper on which mantras and prayers are printed. Old Buddhists usually go to monasteries in the morning, when they walk around the monastery in a clockwise direction while turning prayer wheels with their hands.

Turning a prayer wheel.

Chanting the six-syllable mantra: The six-syllable incantation "Om mani padme hum" is Tibetan Buddhism's most sacred mantra. Tibetan Buddhism considers this six-syllable incantation to be the origin of all things. It is believed that repeated recitation of the six-syllable mantra gathers more merit.

The six-syllable incantation is found written and inscribed in Sanskrit or Tibetan on lintels, ceilings, doorframes, religious artifacts, rocks and other things. In Tibetan-inhabited areas, the six-syllable incantation can be found everywhere, which shows Tibetan people's wishes for a happy future, their devotion to Buddha and their kindness.

Prayer flags (*lungta*): Prayer flags have a triple meaning: first, they have astrological significance; second, those seen fluttering from rooftops, riverbanks, the tops of high mountain passes or any high point are symbols of fate; third, those on the roofs of houses or on mountain tops are the equivalent of sacrificial altars. A typical prayer flag is a square or rectangular piece of colored cloth or paper of between 10 and 60 centimeters in length. A flag pattern consists of five animals in five colors, representing metal, wood, water, fire and earth and indicating a prolonged life. The main subject of the pattern is a flying horse, carrying the three jewels (the Buddha, the dharma and the sangha). In the upper right is an eagle; in the lower right, a lion; in the upper left, a dragon; and in the lower left, a red tiger.

Turning a prayer wheel.

(6) Tibetan Festivals

The following is a list of the major festivals celebrated in Tibetan areas:

Name	Place	Date in the Tibetan lunar calendar
Tibetan New Year	Throughout Tibet	First day of the first month
Mönlam Festival	All big monasteries	Eighth day of the first month
Great Butter Festival	Lhasa	Fifteenth day of the first month
Saga Dawa Festival	Lhasa	Fifteenth day of the fourth month
Horse-Racing Festival	Gyangzê	Eighteenth day of the fourth month
Lingka Festival	Lhasa	First to 15th days of the fifth month
Sunning the Buddha	Tashilhunpo Monastery	Fourteenth to 16th days of the fifth month
Pilgrimages and offerings to the mountain gods	Throughout Tibet	Fourth day of the sixth month
Sholton Festival	Lhasa	First five days of the seventh month
Bathing Festival	Throughout Tibet	First seven days of the seventh month
Ongkor Festival	Throughout Tibetan rural areas	End of the seventh month
Butter-Lamp Festival	Lhasa	Twenty-fifth day of the 10th month
Banishing the Evil Spirits Festival	Lhasa	Twenty-ninth day of the 12th month

The most jubilant and colorful events in Tibetan life are the different festivals that occur throughout the year. The biggest in scale and most unique are the New Year Festival, the Bathing Festival, the Sholton Festival and the Ongkor Festival.

Tibetan New Year: The Tibetan New Year (Losar in Tibetan) is an important festival. On this day, people bid farewell to the old year and welcome in the new. The Tibetan people enshrine in their hearts their memories of the good and bad of the past year and they offer their blessings to the coming year. Tibetan festivals differ from region to region. For instance, the Banishing the Evil Spirits Festival is held on the 29th day of the 12th month in the Tsang region, while sacrificial objects are offered to the mountain gods on New Year's Day in Amdo (the Tibetan areas in Gansu, Qinghai and Sichuan).

Preparations for the Tibetan New Year celebrations start right at the beginning of the 12th month. To express their wishes for a happy new year, men should have their hair cut and women have their hair washed and plaited a couple of days before New Year's Day. Antithetical couplets written on scrolls and New Year pictures can be found on the doors of houses in areas influenced by Han Chinese culture. However, the couplets are written in Tibetan and the pictures feature lions, dragons and tigers, which are auspicious animals for Tibetans.

On New Year's Eve, every household starts deep-frying all types of doughnuts in butter. On the tables, there will be grain dippers filled with barley flour and wheat, small pots of barley seedlings, candy, butter tea and *chang* (barley beer). The head of a sheep decorated with colored butter will also be on display. Any monks living in the home will chant sutras in a chapel on New Year's Eve. On New Year's Day, women get up at dawn to fetch New Year water, the first bucket of water carried home from the river when the stars are shining in the sky. People burn incense to the river god and then take the water home. They believe that the New Year water is the most auspicious water because it is dew from heaven and also the water that the love goddess Tanma sprinkles over the human world. So this water is believed capable of washing away impurity and anxiety and replacing them with purity and happiness. The first woman to fetch the water is considered the most blessed person. A housewife will put the new water into the bowls at the altar as an offering to the gods and then into a washbasin for the family. A little milk is then added to the water in the washbasin. All the members of the family wash themselves with this water according to seniority.

On New Year's Day, rural folk go to the grasslands for horse racing. The winners are given *katag* scarves by respected elders. The horse race is followed by group dances and other performances. Then old balladeers sing folk songs. Other than watching the performances, people do not go visiting on this day.

Each family stays at home on the first and second day of the year. From the third day onward, people begin to visit friends and relatives. The first words they exchange are the greetings "Losar sang" ("Happy New Year") and "Tashi delek" ("Luck and happiness"). On the third day, a ritual is held for unmarried 17-year-old girls. In Tibet, a girl comes of age at 17 and, on that day, wears a splendid dress and jeweled ornaments in her hair like other adult women. She visits friends and relatives, who bless her and give her gifts. From that day on, as an adult, she is allowed to make the acquaintance of young men freely. Entertainment during the New Year festival includes horse and yak racing, group dances, songs, and Tibetan opera.

The exorcising of evil spirits is a necessary ritual before the Tibetan New Year. Tibetans believe that evil spirits are the origin of disasters and diseases, so should be driven away before the New Year. The ritual involves giving discolored *tsampa* (roasted barley flour, stained with the dirt from men's skin) as an offering to ghosts, which are represented by piles of stones, and then exorcising the ghosts with burning straws. At the end of the ritual, people enjoy themselves by singing and dancing around the bonfire of burning straws.

The Mönlam Festival is the climax of the New Year celebrations. The Mönlam prayer festival was started in 409 by Tsongkhapa, the founder of the Gelugpa sect. This festival begins on the third day of the year and ends on the 24th day of the first lunar month. During this period, monks and pilgrims pour into Lhasa, forming an ocean of *kashaya* vestments. Lhasa is full of the smoke of burning incense. Tall poles with prayer flags stand before the Jokhang, which is aglow with thousands of butter lamps. The lamps and golden Buddhist pillars shining in the sunshine add radiance and beauty to each other. A mysterious and solemn religious atmosphere pervades the whole city. The chanting and debating of sutras form the main part of the Mönlam Festival. The grand butter-lamp festival on the evening of the 15th day of the month adds a cheerful atmosphere to Lhasa. Along the Barkor circuit are displayed butter sculptures of various patterns, ranging from plants and animals to symbols of good fortune concerning religious stories and fairy tales. In front of the sculptures are butter lamps. The silvery moonlight and the light of the butter lamps make the butter sculptures look vivid. Mass sporting activities are part of the New Year celebrations and the Mönlam Festival. Such traditional sporting activities as horse racing, archery, wrestling and weight lifting are held in Lhasa from the 25th to the 28th day of the first lunar month. As the winners rejoice and the spectators cheer in chorus, the New Year and Mönlam activities come to an end.

Sholton Festival: The days of the Sholton Festival were originally a time when monks were served yogurt banquets. The festival is said to have been founded by the renowned Buddhist master Atisha in the late 11th century when he was on a summer retreat. According to Buddhist law, the participants at the summer retreat had to stay indoors for several weeks over the summer to avoid killing mosquitoes, other insects, and birds, which are frequent in that season. On the last day of their penance, the participants left the monastery and went down to the plains where the lay people offered them yogurt. After enjoying their feast of yogurt, the retreat participants then let themselves have some fun. This is how the Sholton Festival originated. The festival is generally held on the first five days of the seventh lunar month but the time varies from region to region. In Lhasa, the festival was traditionally held at the Potala, Norbulingka and Drepung monasteries but it is no longer held at the Potala.

During the Sholton Festival in the Norbulingka, people have fun singing and dancing and watch operas. In the Norbulingka itself and the woods outside the park, tents are scattered here and there like mushrooms growing on the meadows. When evening comes, people sing and dance by the campfire to the rhythm of drums. Their singing and dancing is sometimes slow and sometimes energetic. The singers and dancers become intoxicated with the spirit of the festival.

The music, whirling dance steps and melodious singing voices of the opera performers present a grand scene on the Norbulingka stage. The Tibetan opera performances bring each year's Sholton Festival to a climax. People all gather in the park to enjoy the opera.

A giant image of Buddha is displayed during the Sholton Festival in Drepung Monastery, so the festival is also called the Festival of Displaying the Buddha Image. On the evening of the 29th day of the first lunar month, people rush into the monastery to wait for the activities to begin.

"Sunning the Buddha" during the Sholton Festival.

A Tibetan opera performance at the Sholton Festival.

Early in the morning on the 30th day, accompanied by the solemn sound of bugles and the burning of incense, monks carry a huge brocade picture of Buddha to the top of a hill, from where they display the picture. When the huge picture of Buddha is put on display, facing the rising sun in the east, four monks blow horns and pilgrims prostrate themselves in worship before the picture of Buddha. The sound of prayers and horns echoes in the mountain, and the magnificent Buddha image is bathed in golden sunshine.

Bathing Festival: The Bathing Festival is held when the planet Venus appears in the night sky during the seventh lunar month.

From the sixth to the 12th day of the seventh lunar month, everybody in Lhasa goes to the river to wash their body and clothes. According to legend, bathing in this way can cure any kind of illness. Men and women, old and young, all gather in high spirits on the riverbank to observe the age-old custom of bathing outdoors, drinking tea and liquor, and singing and dancing. They bathe and spend the whole day giving their bedding its annual wash. It is believed that bathing in river water can ward off disease and make them healthy. The weeklong festival ends when Venus disappears.

Ongkor Festival: In ancient times, bewildering and perilous natural conditions and changeable weather always threatened Tibetan people's very survival. Ancient Tibetan people believed that the natural disasters that damaged their harvests were brought by deities who had been offended by people's wrongdoing, so people held rituals to offer sacrifices to the gods and to pray for blessings from them. People prayed for a good harvest, a flourishing population, and the well-being of their domesticated animals. This is how the traditional Ongkor festival originated.

A typical Ongkor festival is that held in Kunga Shika (Estate), 80 kilometers east of Lhasa. The ceremony is presided over by a sorcerer, who mediates between humans and the gods. On the first day, led by the sorcerer, people offer liquor to the gods, and sing and dance to entertain and please the gods. On the second day, the inhabitants of each hamlet set off in a procession and make a circuit of all their fields. The procession is led by the sorcerer, who holds a colorful arrow, followed by monks with sutras in their hands, and a band. The sounds of singing, bugles and horns mix with each other. The fields are heavy with the smoke of auspicious incense. Each person holds some ears of highland barley and wheat. At the end of the ceremony, these ears of grain are placed upright on the altar, and everybody prays for a good harvest. Then people entertain themselves with singing and dancing and traditional contests.

Joyous dances at the Ongkor Festival.

Horse-Racing Festival in northern Tibet: The Horse-Racing Festival is a grand traditional festival held in northern Tibet's Nagchu grassland for between five and 15 days during the sixth lunar month, when the weather is

Horse racing.

at its best in northern Tibet. In that month, warm weather replaces cold, harsh and windy days. Green grass and wild flowers make the grassland attractive. People in festival costumes rush to attend the race. Tents are set up one after another. Everybody can take part in the race. The festival is not only a horse race. Instead, it comprises a comprehensive range of sporting activities. In addition to horse races over long and short distances, there are exciting feats of horsemanship, which include picking up scarves from the ground as well as archery and rifle shooting contests, all performed on horseback at full gallop. There is also a distinctive yak race. Tug-of-war, high jump and long jump competitions are also held. The stone-lifting contest is very interesting. The heaviest stone to be lifted weighs about 100 kilograms. The person who can lift the heaviest weight is the winner. There are also theatrical performances, movies, and the recitation

Horse racing.

and singing of the ballad *Gesar* by folk performers. Between the races, there is time for nomads to barter in the general stores.

2. Suggestions for Tourists

Transport: Broadly speaking, there are two ways of getting to Tibet – by air or road. There are several flights a day from Chengdu to Lhasa, as well as flights between Lhasa and other cities, such as Beijing, Chongqing, Guangzhou, Kunming, Shanghai, Xi'an, and Xining. There are also direct flights between Lhasa and Qamdo, and several flights a week between Lhasa and Kathmandu.

By highway, there are two main routes: The Sichuan-Tibet highway between Chengdu and Lhasa, which is 2,413 kilometers long and takes eight to 10 days to travel, and the Qinghai-Tibet highway between Golmud and Lhasa, which is 1,214 kilometers long and passes through the Kunlun and Tanggula mountain ranges at an altitude of 4,000 meters. Golmud can be reached by train and there is a regular daily bus service from

Tibetan girls.

there to Lhasa. The bus normally takes 30 hours to reach Lhasa. There is also the Xinjiang-Tibet highway between Yecheng (Kargilik) in Xinjiang and Burang in Tibet's Ngari region, the Yunnan-Tibet highway between Xiaguan in Yunnan and Markam in Tibet, and the China-Nepal highway between Kathmandu and Lhasa, one of the main routes for foreign tourists.

Health precautions: The air in Tibet is thin because of the region's high altitude. The weather is dry and cold. Tourists may suffer from headaches, insomnia and palpitations. Be sure to have enough rest and avoid catching a cold. Those suffering from the altitude's effects should lie in bed and breathe plenty of oxygen. Hotels generally have oxygen cylinders, which provide convenient and effective treatment of altitude sickness. Travelers are advised to bring medicines such as aminophylline, chlorpromazine, the aspirin compound APC and vitamin C, vitamin B_1 (thiamine) and vitamin B_6 (pyridoxine).

Food: Generally, restaurants serve tasty food. Lhasa's Tibet Tourist Restaurant serves Sichuan-style dishes, while the Lhasa Holiday Inn serves Western-style meals. The Shannan Tsethang Restaurant serves Cantonese food. All restaurants serve buffet meals and Tibetan food. In Lhasa and Shigatse, tourist restaurants serve tasty and inexpensive meals.

Itineraries: Before going on a trip to Tibet, it is very important to choose a suitable itinerary. The following are several practical itineraries.

(1) Lhasa tour (four days and three nights)

The Tibetan capital Lhasa, whose name means "ground of the gods," is Tibet's political, cultural and economic center. With an elevation of 3,650 meters, Lhasa is one of the world's highest cities. It is also known for its sunshine. The temperature can rise to 28 degrees Celsius in summer and drop to minus 14 degrees Celsius in winter. The main sites include the Potala, the "three great monasteries" (Drepung, Ganden and Sera), and the Barkor circuit. Folklore and social customs of Lhasa are also worthy of attention.

Day 1: Arrive in Lhasa in the morning, visit the Norbulingka in the afternoon;

Day 2: Visit the Potala in the morning and the Jokhang Temple in the afternoon;

Day 3: Visit the Drepung and Sera monasteries;

Day 4: Leave Lhasa.

(2) Tsethang to Lhasa (five days and four nights)

Tsethang, the capital of southern Tibet's Shannan region, is at an altitude of 3,551 meters. Its name means "playground." Tsethang is said to have been where Tibetan monkeys became men and it was the cradle of the Tubo Dynasty. Its scenic sites include Yumbulagang (Tibet's first palace), Trandruk Temple (Tibet's first temple), Samye Monastery (Tibet's first monastery), the Tombs of the Tibetan Kings, Lhamoi Lhatso Lake and Yamdrok Lake.

Day 1: Arrive in Tsethang, visit the Tombs of the Tibetan Kings and Trandruk Temple, stay overnight in Tsethang;

Day 2: Visit Samye Monastery, leave Tsethang for Lhasa, stay overnight in Lhasa;

Day 3: Visit the Potala in the morning and the Jokhang Temple and Barkor circuit in the afternoon, stay overnight in Lhasa;

Day 4: Visit Drepung and Sera monasteries, stay overnight in Lhasa;

Day 5: Leave Lhasa.

(3) Lhasa to Tsethang (six days and five nights)

Day 1: Arrive in Lhasa, visit the Norbulingka, stay overnight in Lhasa;

Day 2: Visit the Potala in the morning and the Jokhang Temple and Barkor circuit in the afternoon, stay overnight in Lhasa;

Day 3: Visit the Drepung and Sera monasteries and the Hospital of Tibetan Medicine, stay overnight in Lhasa;

Day 4: Leave Lhasa for Tsethang, visit the Tombs of the Tibetan Kings, Trandruk Temple and Yumbulagang, stay overnight in Tsethang;

Day 5: Visit Samye Monastery;

Day 6: Leave Tsethang.

(4) Lhasa and Shigatse (six days and five nights)

Shigatse is in southern Tibet, north of the Himalayas and more than 300 kilometers from Lhasa, at the point where the Yarlung Zangbo and Nyang Qu rivers converge. It is more than 3,800 meters above sea level at its lowest point and 6,646 meters at its highest point. Climatically, it is a semiarid monsoon highland temperate zone. The temperature can rise to 21 degrees Celsius in summer and drop to minus 12 degrees Celsius in winter. The name Shigatse means "the best manor." It is the seat of the Panchen Lama. The town is the seat of Shigatse Prefecture. The main scenic spots include Tashilhunpo Monastery (the main monastery of Panchen Erdeni), Shalu Monastery, Palkhor Chode and Sakya Monastery, as well as Gyangzê Fortress, a center of defense against British aggression. Mountaineers could go to the Qomolangma (Everest) base camp in Dingri.

Day 1: Arrive in Lhasa and visit the Norbulingka;

Day 2: Visit the Potala in the morning and the Jokhang Temple and Barkor circuit in the afternoon;

Day 3: Visit the Drepung and Sera monasteries and the Hospital of Tibetan Medicine;

Day 4: Leave Lhasa for Shigatse, visit Tashilhunpo Monastery, stay overnight in Shigatse;

Day 5: Leave Shigatse for Lhasa, visiting natural beauty spots on the way, and stay overnight in Lhasa;

Day 6: Leave Lhasa.

(5) Lhasa to Gyangzê and Shigatse (seven days and six nights)

Day 1: Arrive in Lhasa and visit the Norbulingka or take a rest;

Day 2: Visit the Potala in the morning and the Jokhang Temple and Barkor circuit in the afternoon;

Day 3: Visit the Drepung and Sera monasteries and the Hospital of Tibetan Medicine;

Day 4: Leave Lhasa for Gyangzê, visit Yamdrok Lake, Snow-Mountains and Palkhor Chode Monastery, stay overnight in Gyangzê;

Day 5: Leave Gyangzê for Shigatse, visit Tashilhunpo Monastery, the carpet factory and agricultural market, stay overnight in Shigatse;

Day 6: Leave Shigatse for Lhasa, visit natural beauty spots on the way, stay overnight in Lhasa;

Day 7: Leave Lhasa.

(6) Lhasa to Ngari (about 23 days and 22 nights)

The region of Ngari is in western Tibet. On its south and west, it borders Nepal, India and Kashmir, with the Himalayas between them. Its capital town is Shiquanhe (Gar), which is 1,586 kilometers from Lhasa and 1,085 kilometers from Yecheng in Xinjiang. Generally speaking, Ngari is accessible only in summer. The average temperature in July is 12 degrees Celsius. Ngari has been described as the "roof of the roof of the world". Some people say that nobody can discover the real Tibet without going to Ngari. Snow-covered mountains, icy rivers, grasslands, deserts, rivers, lakes, forests and wild animals provide magnificent natural scenery. The site of the Guge kingdom, Toling Monastery, stone caves and rock paintings are great creations of the ancient highland people. Mount Kangrinboqê (Mount Kailas) and the lake Mapham Yumco (Manasarovar) are sacred places visited by tourists.

Itinerary from Lhasa to Ngari and then back to Lhasa:

Lhasa, Shigatse, Sangsang, Coqên, Gêrzê, Shiquanhe (Gar), Rutog, Zanda, Barga, Zhongba, Saga, Gyirong, Dingri, Sa'gya, Shigatse, Gyangzê, Lhasa.

Tibet Tourism Bureau telephone and fax numbers:

Beijing office	Tel: (+86) (010) 6593 6538	Fax: (+86) (010) 6593 6538
Chengdu office	Tel: (+86) (028) 333 3988 ext 229	Fax: (+86) (028) 334 7048
Shanghai office	Tel: (+86) (021) 6228 8845	Fax: (+86) (021) 6274 8488
Xi'an office	Tel: (+86) (029) 526 1980	Fax: (+86) (029) 526 1027
Hong Kong office	Tel: (+852) 2838 3391	Fax: (+852) 2834 1535
Japan office (Tokyo)	Tel: (+81) (03) 3639 3119	Fax: (+81) (03) 3639 3896
Nepal office (Kathmandu)	Tel: (+977) (1) 410 411	Fax: (+977) (1) 227 538
United States office (Pomona, California)	Tel: (001) (909) 629 8888	Fax: (001) (909) 629 8889

图书在版编目（CIP）数据

西藏的历史与人文景观 / 王钦格勒，陈庆英著.
－北京：外文出版社，2006
ISBN 7-119-04203-3

I. 西… II. ①王… ②陈… III. ①西藏－地方史 ② 名胜古迹－简介－西藏
IV.K297.5：K928.707.5

中国版本图书馆 CIP 数据核字（2005）第 098599 号

英文翻译	陈观胜	李培茱
英文审定	贺 军	
图片提供	陈庆英 李文慧 熊文彬 虞向军	
中文编辑	杨春燕	
装帧设计	蔡 荣	
印刷监制	冯 浩	

西藏的历史与人文景观

王钦格勒　陈庆英　著

*

© 外文出版社
外文出版社出版
（中国北京百万庄大街 24 号）
邮政编码　100037
外文出版社网址 http://www.flp.com.cn
外文出版社电子信箱：info@flp.com.cn
sales@flp.com.cn
北京京都六环印刷厂印刷
中国国际图书贸易总公司发行
（中国北京车公庄西路 35 号）
北京邮政信箱第 399 号　邮政编码　100044
2006 年（大 32 开）第 1 版
2006 年第 1 版第 1 次印刷
（英）
ISBN 7-119-04203-3
07200
11-E-3698P